A Small Town in Syria

A Small Town in Syria

Ottoman Hama in the Eighteenth and Nineteenth Centuries

James A. Reilly

PETER LANG
Oxford · Bern · Berlin · Bruxelles · Frankfurt am Main · New York · Wien

Die Deutsche Bibliothek – CIP-Einheitsaufnahme

Reilly, James A.:
A small town in Syria : Ottoman Hama in the Eighteenth and Nineteenth centuries / James A. Reilly. – Oxford ; Bern ; Berlin ; Bruxelles ; Frankfurt am Main ; New York ; Wien : Lang, 2002
ISBN 3-906766-90-X

British Library and Library of Congress Cataloguing-in-Publication Data: A catalogue record for this book is available from The British Library, Great Britain, and from The Library of Congress, USA

Cover illustration: Watercolor of Hama, done in the 1930s by the Danish artist Ejnar Fugmann. Oriented northward, the illustration depicts the Kaylani complex on the banks of the Orontes, with Jisr al-Shaykh to the left and the Citadel Hill in the distance.

Source: P. J. Riis, Hama: Danske arkœlogers udgravninger i Syrien 1930–38, *published by Rhodos in Copenhagen, 1987, ISBN 87-7245-209-9. The illustration is reproduced with the publisher's permission.*

Cover design: Thomas Jaberg, Peter Lang AG

ISBN 3-906766-90-X
US-ISBN 0-8204-5606-3

Contents

Maps

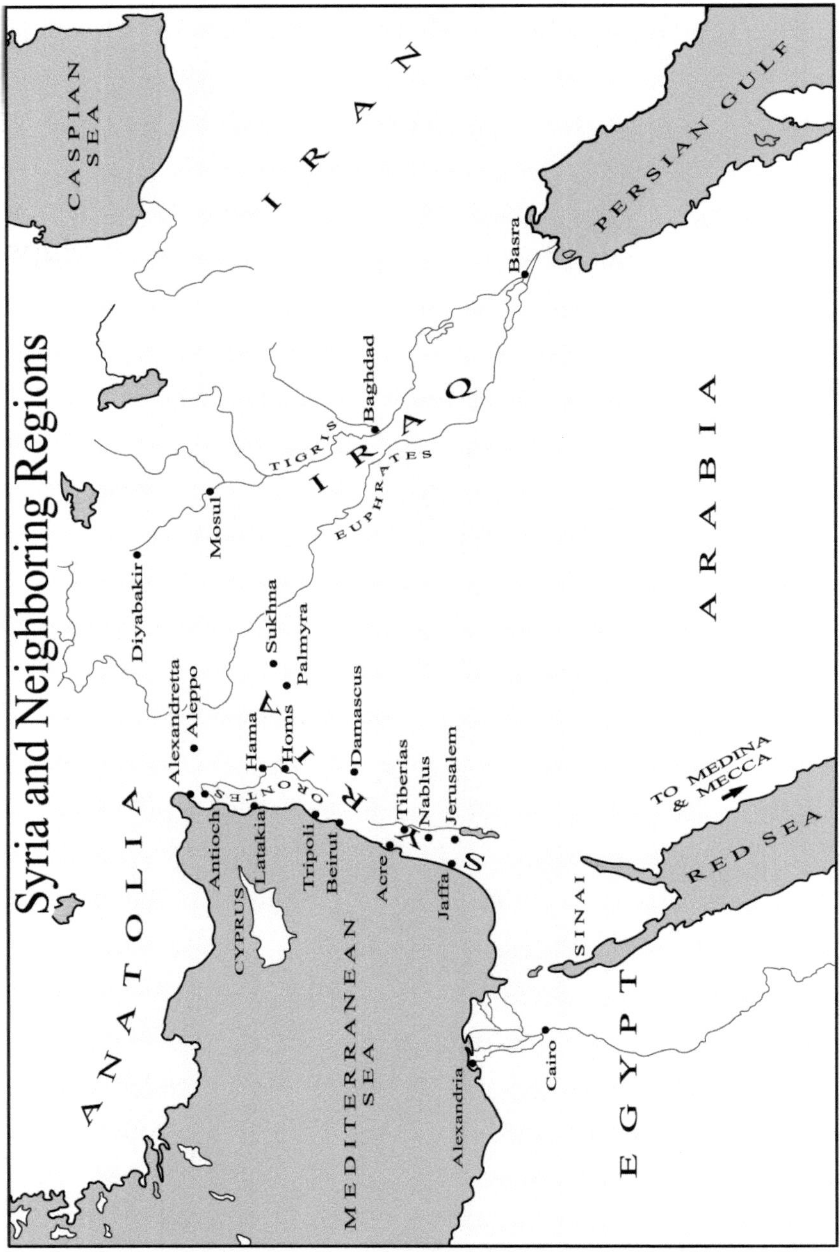
Syria and Neighboring Regions
CASPIAN SEA
IRAN
PERSIAN GULF
Basra
Baghdad
IRAQ
TIGRIS
EUPHRATES
Mosul
Diyabakir
Sukhna
Palmyra
Alexandretta
Aleppo
Hama
Homs
Damascus
ORONTES
SYRIA
Tiberias
Nablus
Jerusalem
ANATOLIA
Antioch
Latakia
Tripoli
Beirut
Acre
Jaffa
CYPRUS
MEDITERRANEAN SEA
ARABIA
TO MEDINA & MECCA
RED SEA
SINAI
EGYPT
Cairo
Alexandria

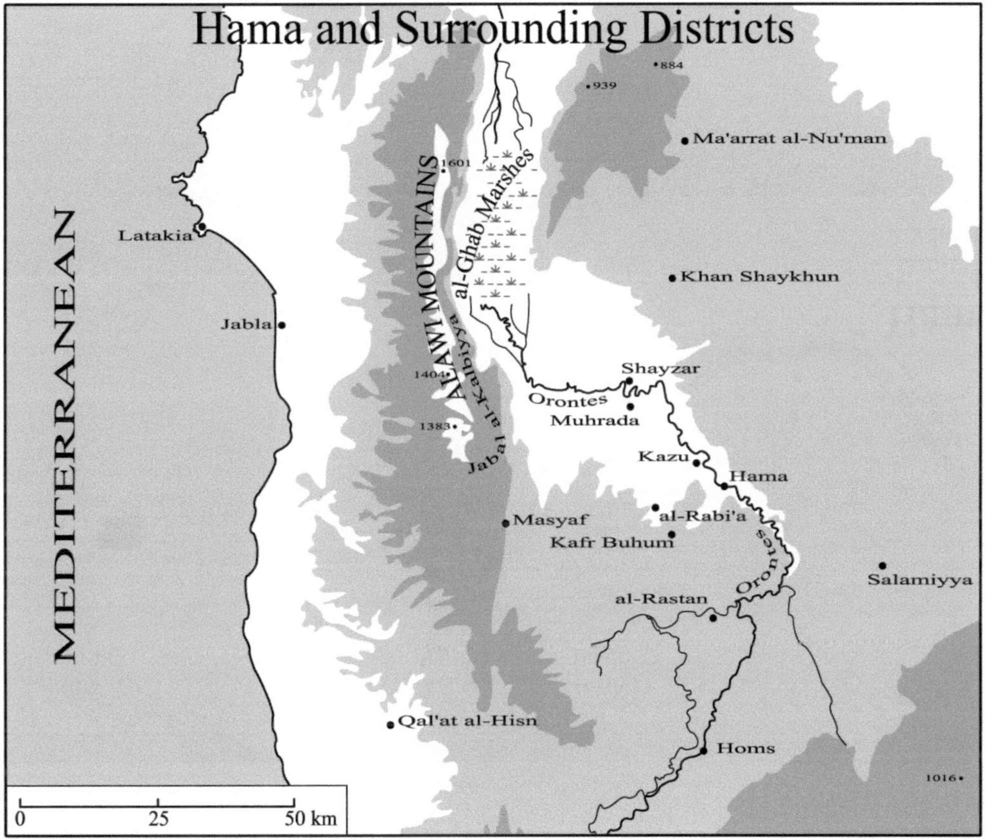
Hama and Surrounding Districts
MEDITERRANEAN
Latakia
Jabla
ALAWI MOUNTAINS
al-Ghab Marshes
Jabal al-Kalbiyya
1601
1404
1383
939
884
Ma'arrat al-Nu'man
Khan Shaykhun
Shayzar
Orontes
Muhrada
Kazu
Hama
Masyaf
al-Rabi'a
Kafr Buhum
Salamiyya
al-Rastan
Qal'at al-Hisn
Homs
1016
0
25
50 km

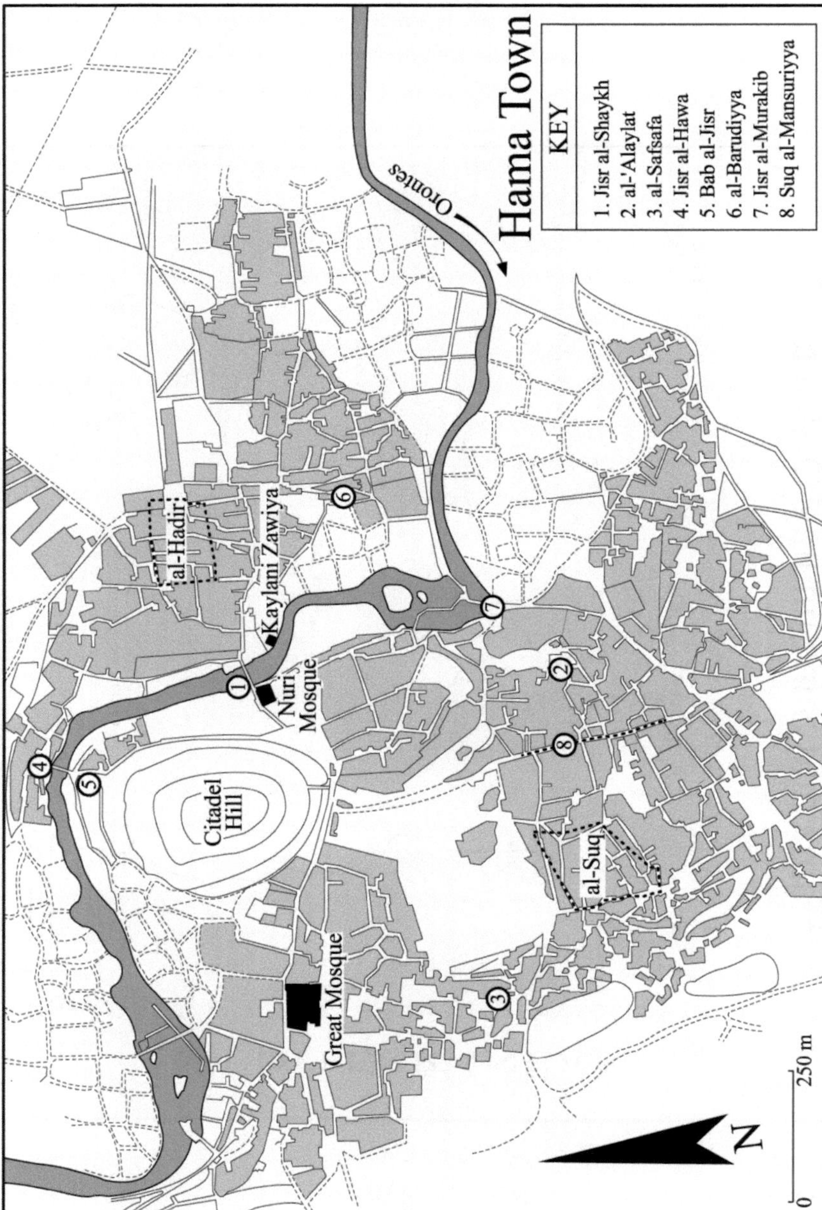

Hama Town
KEY
1. Jisr al-Shaykh
2. al-'Alaylat
3. al-Safsafa
4. Jisr al-Hawa
5. Bab al-Jisr
6. al-Barudiyya
7. Jisr al-Murakib
8. Suq al-Mansuriyya
Orontes
al-Hadir
Kaylani Zawiya
Nuri Mosque
Citadel Hill
Great Mosque
al-Suq
N
0
250 m

Acknowledgements

I have incurred many debts over the years as I studied Ottoman Syria and eventually came to write this work. First of all there were my teachers at the American University of Beirut and at Georgetown University who sparked and encouraged my interest in Middle Eastern and Arab history. At AUB they included Samir Seikaly, Kamal Salibi, the late Marwan Buheiry, and the late Hanna Batatu. At Georgetown they included John Ruedy, Thomas M. Ricks and Hisham Sharabi. In addition, Judith Tucker provided assistance and support in the latter stages of my dissertation writing. While researching in Damascus I received help and encouragement from Abdul-Karim Rafeq and Mme Daad Hakim, who made the Damascus archives comprehensible and accessible, respectively. Without their ongoing assistance and encouragement this research would have been difficult indeed. Also in Damascus, the staff at Mme Hakim's Historic Documents Center, at the Institut Français d'Etudes Arabes, and the United States Information Service offered their facilities and their hospitality. Professor Kassem Toueir at the Syrian Directorate of Antiquities and Museums facilitated my applications for research permission. Other friends and associates in and around the Damascus archives included Randi Deguilhem, Margaret Lee Meriwether, Abd al-Razzaq Moaz, and Gerd Winkelhane. Later, Linda Schilcher helped to broaden my scholarly contacts through the Syrian Studies Association and she shared with me her material on the 'Azm family. At various times I worked at the Public Records Office in Britain and the French Foreign Ministry archives, and I am grateful for the assistance that I received from their staffs.

Major research funding for this book came from the Fulbright-Hayes program of the United States government, and the Canadian government's Social Sciences and Humanities Research Council. The U.S. National Endowment for the Humanities also provided assistance. I appreciate the support that I have received over the years from my employer, the University of Toronto, and from colleagues in Toronto's Department of Near and Middle Eastern Civilizations. A special note of thanks is due to Kurt Wegner, who prepared the maps for this publication; to Ryan Gingeras, who compiled the index; and to Graham Speake and Joanna Turner of Peter Lang publishers, who helped me to turn a typescript into a publishable book. Errors or shortcomings that readers may find between these covers are solely the author's responsibility, of course.

The greatest personal debts are owed to my family. My mother and father encouraged my academic pursuits, and I was able to study in Washington and Beirut only through repeated recourse to the parental purse. My wife Sabah Ghazzawi put up with the travels and travails that my research and career have demanded. Finally, our son Kamal is an ongoing and joyful reminder of the really important things in life.

Toronto, January 2002

Chapter One: Introduction

This study of the Syrian town of Hama in the Ottoman period grows out of two interrelated concerns. One is a wish to trace some of the ways in which the global changes of the nineteenth century affected a particular region and locale. Therefore the study looks into the actions and responses of local people – corporate groups, classes and institutions – with respect to the major transformations associated with Middle Eastern state-formation and Syria's integration into the capitalist world economy. The second concern of this study is to reconstruct and portray some of the patterns and complexities of local society. How Middle Eastern societies functioned and worked in Ottoman times, and how people lived their lives, is better understood now than it was a quarter century ago. A generation of historians has invested many years in the exploitation of local judicial archives. They have attempted to tell stories of the Middle East 'from the inside' by relying less exclusively than did many of their predecessors on sources and documents external to the region.[1] Pioneers who pointed the way for a subsequent generation of scholars include André Raymond and Abdul-Karim Rafeq.[2] In the wake of their studies based on judicial archives, a more nuanced understanding of Ottoman-Arab societies has become possible. This current of research has not yet run its course, as recent studies focusing on particular quarters of Ottoman Damascus attest.[3]

1 Randi Deguilhem, thematic conversation presentation, 33rd annual meeting of the Middle East Studies Association, Washington DC, 19–22 November 1999.

2 André Raymond, *Artisans et commerçants au Caire au XVIIIe siècle*, 2 vols. (Damascus, 1973–1974); Abdul-Karim Rafeq ['Abd al-Karim Rafiq], *Buhuth fi al-Tarikh al-Iqtisadi wa-al-Ijtima'i li-Bilad al-Sham fi al-'Asr al-Hadith* (Damascus, 1985).

3 Brigitte Marino, *Le Faubourg du Midan à Damas à l'époque ottomane: espace urbain, société et habitat (1742–1830)* (Damascus, 1997); Toru Miura, "Personal Networks surrounding the Salihiyya Court in 19th Century

Given the urban bias of available sources, historical research on Ottoman Syria has tended to focus on the major inland centers of Damascus and Aleppo and the religiously important center of Jerusalem.[4] These studies have developed a number of themes about Ottoman-Syrian urban institutions and structures. Among these themes are the importance of craft corporations, the competition and symbiosis between local notables and Ottoman-linked military elites, and competition for access to the fiscal resources of town and country. The institutions, laws, and social dynamics of Ottoman Syria were complex, and a variegated series of relationships developed between and among local, regional, and imperial forces. Moreover, generalizations applicable to the older interior centers are not necessarily valid for rapidly developing port towns of the nineteenth century such as Beirut.[5]

The present study of Hama offers a picture of another Syrian town and its region. Based principally on a sampling of local archival materials, this book cannot entirely represent a 'view from within,' given lacunae in the local judicial records and the existence of pertinent and valuable data from the usual suspects – namely European consular and travelers' reports. Nevertheless this study does suggest patterns and relationships that shaped the lives of Hamawis (people of Hama) in the eighteenth and nineteenth centuries. It communicates some of the complexities of Hama's society, and the ways in which its

---

Damascus," in *Espace et société dans les villes arabes du Machreq à l'époque ottomane* (Damascus, in press).

4 E.g. Colette Establet and Jean-Paul Pascual, *Familles et fortunes à Damas: 450 foyers damascains en 1700* (Damascus, 1994); Zouhair Ghazzal, *L'Economie politique de Damas durant le XIXe siècle: structures traditionelles et capitalisme* (Damascus, 1993); Bruce Masters, *The Origins of Western Economic Dominance in the Middle East: Mercantilism and the Islamic Economy in Aleppo, 1600–1750* (New York, 1988); Abraham Marcus, *The Middle East on the Eve of Modernity: Aleppo in the Eighteenth Century* (New York, 1989); Amnon Cohen, *Economic Life in Ottoman Jerusalem* (Cambridge UK, 1989); Dror Ze'evi, *An Ottoman Century: The District of Jerusalem in the 1600s* (Albany, 1996).

5 Cf. Leila Tarazi Fawaz, *Merchants and Migrants in Nineteenth-Century Beirut* (Cambridge MA, 1983).

local realities intersected and interacted with the 'big changes' of the later Ottoman period.[6]

Sources

Social historians of Ottoman Syria draw heavily on the *shari'a* (Islamic law) court registers of the various towns and cities of geographic Syria. This book follows suit. The major part of its data are drawn from three registers of the Hama law courts,[7] registers whose contents are separated by intervals of some 50–60 years: vol. 42 (1727–1734), vol. 46 (1788–1800), and vol. 53 (1849–1852). Although this selective approach means that material from intervening volumes and decades is passed over, the volumes used do represent the particular periods from which they are drawn. Comparing them with each other enables us to treat a 125-year period in Hama on the basis of court records. These have been supplemented by the use of Arabic literary accounts, French and British travelers' narratives, and European consular reports. The latter are primarily useful for the period after 1850 when France in particular developed an interest in the economic possibilities of Hama and its region.

Shari'a court registers have at times been treated as objective documentary sources from which researchers can extract reasonably reliable data in order to reconstruct historical structures and patterns. Such an assumption is tempting to embrace because the registers contain information about social and economic history that is difficult or impossible to find elsewhere, and historians' understanding of the Ottoman lands has been greatly enhanced by their judicious use. Like

---

6 Judith E. Tucker, "Taming the West: Trends in the Writing of Arab Social History in Anglophone Academia," in *Theory, Politics, and the Arab World: Critical Responses*, ed. Hisham Sharabi (New York, 1990), 198–227.

7 See Vladimir Glasman, "Les documents du tribunal religieux de Hama: leur importance pour la connaissance de la vie quotidienne dans une petite ville de la Syrie centrale à l'époque ottomane," in *Les Villes dans l'Empire ottoman: activités et sociétés*, ed. Daniel Panzac (Paris, 1991), 17–39.

all sources, however, the law-court registers have their built-in biases and limitations. The registers reveal only those social processes and transactions that came under the purview of the local administration and for which a judicial record was deemed useful or necessary. The scribes who produced the registers had their own criteria for including or excluding information, and they reflected the values and assumptions of the system in which they worked.[8] This caveat notwithstanding, the Hama registers are an essential source. Hama's literary output during the two centuries under consideration was meager compared to that of a major center like Damascus.[9] Hama's law court registers are therefore by default a unique documentary record of the town's history.[10]

The urban bias of the law-court registers is reflected in the Hama series. Before construction of an intrusive modern bureaucracy concerned with administration of rural life, much of importance that occurred in the countryside escaped the notice of court scribes and consequently of later historians who draw upon their work. Rural people were deterred from using the *shari'a* court due to the physical distance separating town from village, the fees required of litigants, a presumed preference for the customary and the familiar, and (in the case of disputes between people of unequal status or power) fear of possible retribution. Despite their mass of detail, the Hama registers offer only sporadic and incomplete glimpses into the organization of

---

8 Khalid Ziyada, *al-Sura al-Taqlidiyya li-al-Mujtama' al-Madani: Qira'a Manhajiyya fi Sijillat Mahkamat Tarabulus al-Shar'iyya fi al-Qarn al-Sabi' 'Ashar wa-Bidayat al-Qarn al-Thamin 'Ashar* (Tripoli [Lebanon], 1983), 28–29, 33, 43–53; Najwa al-Qattan, "The Historian at the Shari'a Court: Judging the Evidence Concerning Legal Practice," paper presented at the 29th Annual Meeting of the Middle East Studies Association of North America, Washington DC, Dec. 1995.

9 A local history of the later Ottoman period, written in the first decade of the twentieth century, bemoans Hama's low cultural level of the time. Al-Shaykh Ahmad al-Sabuni, *Tarikh Hamah* (Hama, 1956), 118.

10 The central Ottoman archives are a potential source for the study of Hama as well. However, the only published work in this vein to date has been Mehmet Ibsirli, "A Preliminary Study of the Public Waqfs in Homs and Hama in the XVIth Century," in *Studies on Turkish-Arab Relations Annual* (Istanbul, 1986), 119–147.

land tenure, and they tell us almost nothing about matters such as internal village structures, inter-village relations, relations between villagers and pastoralists, and widely accepted but unarticulated societal norms. At best, historians can use the court registers to get some idea of what urban elites and notables thought was happening in the countryside, or (less often) what villagers wanted urban authorities to know.

Nevertheless, and despite these limitations of and problems with the source material, using the court registers to explore Hama in the later Ottoman period is both possible and useful. They allow historians to make plausible generalizations about the fabric of urban life and urban-rural relations. This study begins with a consideration of Hama's families and social networks, goes on to treat land tenure, and concludes with an account of Hama's production and trade in the eighteenth and nineteenth centuries. Throughout it will place Hama in a wider Syrian context.

Geographic Syria (Arabic Bilad al-Sham) – an area that encompasses the western Fertile Crescent – has a long history of urban settlement. Jericho is reputed to have been the first town ever built; Jerusalem's status as a city of great religious significance stretches back for millennia; and Damascus and Aleppo vie for the title of 'oldest continuously inhabited city in the world.' Syrian towns owe their location and longevity to the availability of water, and their location along ancient routes of trade and communication. The importance of towns and cities to Syria is shown by the extent of the country's urbanization: in the early nineteenth century, some one-fifth of geographic Syria's population lived in towns and cities, a remarkably high proportion for a pre-industrial, predominantly agrarian society. (In contrast, for example, only about ten percent of the Egyptian population at about the same time is estimated to have lived in towns and cities.)[11] Syrian rural areas and market towns were linked to regional and international circuits of trade via the great interior

11 Charles Issawi, *The Economic History of the Middle East 1800–1914* (Chicago, 1966), 220; idem, "Economic Change and Urbanization in the Middle East," in *Middle Eastern Cities: Ancient, Islamic, and Contemporary Middle Eastern Urbanism*, ed. Ira M. Lapidus (Berkeley, 1969), 102.

centers of Aleppo and Damascus, or through seaports such as Tripoli and Saida. Thus Ottoman Syria in the early modern period can be visualized as a hierarchical network of regional economies. The markets and produce of rural areas were tied to regional centers, which were themselves connected in turn to seaports or major inland cities that functioned as 'dry ports' opening onto the trade routes of the steppe and desert.[12] Prior to the nineteenth century the major centers of Ottoman administration in Syria were the inland cities of Aleppo and Damascus, as well as the ports of Tripoli and Saida. Among them was divided responsibility for the administration and taxation of the country.

In the early 1980s historian Antoine Abdel Nour noted that economic activities and exchanges among the Arab cities of the first rank were relatively well known, but that corresponding information and studies for secondary towns were lacking.[13] In the years since, the historiography of Syria has reached a point where smaller inland towns are receiving attention.[14] The present book adds to this literature. It portrays key aspects of the social and economic structure of one such secondary town, Hama, during the later phases of Ottoman rule in the eighteenth and nineteenth centuries. The patterns of wealth and power found in Hama recall generalizations about the importance of family alliances and social networks in the functioning of larger Ottoman-Syrian inland cities.[15] In turn, the relationship between Ottoman center and Syrian periphery created a distinct type of urban

---

12 Antoine Abdel Nour, *Introduction à l'histoire urbaine de la Syrie ottomane (XVIe–XVIIIe siècle)* (Beirut, 1982), 262–264; Dominique Chevallier, *Villes et travail en Syrie du XIXe au XXe siècle* (Paris, 1982), 38.

13 Abdel Nour, *Introduction*, 263.

14 The most notable study of this type to date is Beshara Doumani, *Rediscovering Palestine: Merchants and Peasants in Jabal Nablus, 1700–1900* (Berkeley, 1995). A recent book that draws many of its examples from Hama is Dick Douwes, *The Ottomans in Syria: A History of Justice and Oppression* (London and New York, 2000).

15 Cf. Margaret L. Meriwether, *The Kin Who Count: Family and Society in Ottoman Aleppo, 1770–1840* (Austin, 1999); and Linda Schatkowski Schilcher, *Families in Politics: Damascene Factions and Estates in the 18th and 19th Centuries* (Stuttgart, 1985).

society whose cultural and political legacy survived the demise of the Ottoman empire and France's creation of the modern Syrian state after the First World War.[16]

Hama is located on the Orontes river (Nahr al-'Asi), 200 kilometers north of Damascus and 75 kilometers east of the Mediterranean coast from which it is separated by a rugged chain of mountains, the 'Alawi range. Known as Hamath in ancient times, the town owes its 3000-year history of recorded human settlement to the fresh running water of the Orontes, and to its location along major caravan and trade routes. Hama sits astride the passage from Aleppo to Damascus, the principal conduit for people, goods, and money in Syria in Ottoman times as well as today. The only potential competitor to the north–south route from Aleppo to Damascus was Syria's coastal plain, running west of and parallel to the line of hills and mountains that overlook the Mediterranean from Antioch in the north to Acre and Jaffa in the south. However, Syria's coastal cities had been devastated and depopulated in the Middle Ages as a consequence of the Crusades, and until the seventeenth century the ports of Tripoli and Saida were sentry outposts guarding the interior rather than significant north–south relay stations.[17] Hence Hama was an important stop on Syria's major trunk road, a busy transit point for caravans and soldiers during the Ottoman epoch.

A promontory that rises above Hama made the site defensible, and its medieval citadel was perched atop it. (Today only faint traces of the citadel can be seen, since the fortress's remaining buildings and walls were cannibalized for building materials in the middle period of Ottoman rule.)[18] A distinguishing feature of Hama was (and is) its assembly of wooden water wheels whose design goes back to classical antiquity. These wheels lift water from the Orontes to the higher ground on either side of the river and allow for a verdant band of cultivation. Poets celebrated Hama's gardens and water wheels, which

---

16 Philip S. Khoury, *Syria and the French Mandate: The Politics of Arab Nationalism 1920–1945* (Princeton, 1987), 619.

17 Abdel Nour, *Introduction*, 305–313; 350–355.

18 'Ali Musa and Muhammad Harba, *Muhafazat Hamah: Dirasa Tabi'iyya-Tarikhiyya-Bashariyya-Iqtisadiyya* (Damascus, 1985), 93.

remained its trademark over the centuries.[19] Hama and its riparian neighbor Homs some 55 kilometers upstream were renowned for their fertility, evident in springtime when crops and cultivation extended from one horizon to the other on the Homs-Hama plain.[20]

Syria came under Muslim Arab rule in the seventh century. Though the end of Christian Byzantine government marked a dramatic political rupture, the onset of Muslim rule did not traumatize the lives of the Syrian population. Their new Arab masters were in many respects more akin to them than the Hellenistic rulers of Byzantium had been. Within a relatively short period of time Syrians forsook the Aramaic language and adopted Arabic. The majority came to accept Islam as well, though Muslim tolerance ensured that Christianity continued to be publicly and widely professed.

Hama was not particularly prominent during the early centuries of Muslim rule. Unlike Homs, Hama had not been the site of a major battle between the early Muslims and Byzantium so it did not acquire comparable luster in Muslim historiography and legend. Hama knew no parallel to the Muslim shrines of Homs that were built around the tomb of the Arab conqueror of Syria, Khalid ibn al-Walid, and the Companions of the Prophet who had marched northward with him.[21]

The advent of the Crusades (eleventh–thirteenth centuries) increased Hama's importance in the Islamic period. Hama became a redoubt of Muslim rulers who confronted the Frankish principalities along the Syrian littoral. After Sultan Nur al-Din Zengi consolidated his rule in Damascus (1154), he built a hospice (*bimaristan*) and an

---

19 Cf. ʻAbd al-Ghani al-Nabulsi, *al-Haqiqa wa-al-Majaz fi al-Rihla ila Bilad al-Sham wa-Misr wa-al-Hijaz* (Cairo, 1986), 46–48; and Jacques Weulersse, *L'Oronte: étude de flueve* (Tours, 1940), 57.

20 Cf. Mikha'il Mishaqa, *Muntakhabat min al-Jawab ʻala Iqtirah al-Ahbab*, 2nd ed., ed. Asad Rustum and Subhi Abu Shaqra (Beirut, 1985), 143; Gertrude L. Bell, *Syria: The Desert and the Sown* (London, 1907), 224; Muhammad ʻAli Basha, *al-Rihla al-Shamiyya* (Beirut, 1981), 140.

21 Many quarters in the old city of Homs contain tombs attributed to Companions of the Prophet and to other early converts to Islam. Na'im Salim al-Zahrawi, *Usur Hims wa-Amakin al-ʻIbada min khuruj Ibrahim Pasha al-Misri wa-hatta khuruj al-ʻUthmaniyyin al-Atrak, 1840–1918. Dirasa Watha'iqiyya* (Homs, 1995), vol. 2, *passim*.

eponymous mosque in Hama, the latter of which remains a landmark to the present day. The Ayyubid descendants of Salah al-Din (Saladin), Nur al-Din's deputy and successor, established a local dynasty in Hama in 1178–1179 before submitting to the Egyptian-based Mamluk sultans from the 1250s onward.[22] The most illustrious of these Ayyubid princes was the author Abu al-Fida (d. 1331), whose reign was later memorialized as Hama's 'golden age.'[23] Finally, with the Ottoman conquest of the country in 1516, Hama and other Syrian towns were incorporated into a vast political and economic framework that determined the final shape of their pre-modern character.

The Ottoman conquest had been precipitated by frontier and trade disputes with the Mamluk sultans of Cairo. From an early period the Ottoman rulers in Istanbul had recognized the strategic and commercial importance of Syria, mastery of which offered them access to the riches and holy places of Egypt and Arabia. These latter were, in turn, gateways to the Indian Ocean whose historic trade networks were succumbing to European control beginning with the Portuguese at the turn of the sixteenth century. Therefore the Ottomans' occupation of Syria in 1516, at the moment when their Empire was approaching the peak of its powers, had both strategic and commercial implications.[24]

The Ottoman sultans had built up a vast body of military and bureaucratic servants who administered extensive areas of south-eastern Europe, the Black Sea littoral and Anatolia in addition to Arabic-speaking lands of the Middle East and most of North Africa. Ottoman priorities were defense of the frontiers, security of trade routes, and prompt remission of taxes. A legally defined ruling class – the sultan and his household plus the thousands of soldiers and administrators in his service – were distinct from the subject population (*ra'aya*) on whom the tax burden fell. Ottoman rule in newly conquered regions was in the first instance conservative and it adapted

---

22 *Encyclopedia of Islam* (EI), 2nd ed., s.v. "Hamât" by D. Sourdel.

23 Ahmad Ghassan Sabanu, *Mamlakat Hamah al-Ayyubiyya* (Damascus, 1984), 113–131.

24 On the Ottoman conquest of Syria see P. M. Holt, *Egypt and the Fertile Crescent 1516–1922: A Political History* (Ithaca, 1966), chap. 2.

itself to pre-existing social, economic, and political structures. This conservatism notwithstanding, new configurations of power gradually emerged in the Ottoman Syrian provinces. Successive fiscal and political crises in the late sixteenth and early seventeenth centuries compelled Istanbul's representatives in Syria to ally themselves with various local forces in order better to ensure the overall objectives of defense, internal security, and tax remission. Such alliances served to break down the heretofore clear distinction between the rulers and those whom they ruled. As early as the seventeenth century, local dynasties emerged in parts of Syria and Palestine under the aegis and at the sufferance of the Ottoman state. This devolution or sharing of power, though in one sense a symptom of Ottoman 'weakening,' also gave the Ottoman center a high degree of flexibility. The Ottomans were able to work with and to manipulate local forces in a manner that allowed a durable political framework to endure in the Arab Middle East for four centuries. Notables and elites, though locally and regionally based, were encouraged to identify themselves with Istanbul and to look to the Porte (the Ottoman government) for legitimization and political support.[25]

The first 150 years of Ottoman rule were good ones in the main for the cities and towns of Syria. The Syrian lands were integrated into trade routes that spanned the length and breadth of the Mediterranean, the Indian Ocean via Egypt and Arabia, the Black Sea region via Istanbul, and Iran via Iraq and eastern Anatolia. Public works in the form of pious endowments (sing. *waqf*, pl. *awqaf*) helped to spur the creation of new quarters in Aleppo and Damascus and to improve the infrastructure of Jerusalem. Ottoman officialdom took a keen interest in trade and the development of trading infrastructure, in particular caravansaries. Security threats to urban Syrian commercial interests were internal, mostly taking the form of highwaymen, brigands or rebels from disaffected portions of rural peasant and pastoralist communities. The Ottomans' foreign enemies were far away, in Iran, Hungary, and north of the Black Sea. Only in Jerusalem, for a time,

25 Albert Hourani, *A History of the Arab Peoples* (New York, 1992), 214–220; Abdul-Rahim Abu-Husayn, *Provincial Leaderships in Syria 1575–1650* (Beirut, 1985), *passim*; Ze'evi, *Ottoman Century*, *passim*.

did the fear of a new crusade lead to reinforcement of the city's fortifications. Elsewhere in Syria, including Hama, citadels and walls were allowed to deteriorate or they became incorporated into the domestic urban fabric, illustrating a general insouciance regarding the possibility of outside invasion or attack. Syria settled securely within the confines of the Ottoman state.[26]

Hama shared in this general well-being during the sixteenth and seventeenth centuries. Its built-up area expanded with the growth of regional trade and the intensification of links between the town and its countryside. Whilst Hama suffered a setback toward the end of the sixteenth century during the period of Ottoman troubles associated with the Celali military rebellions, Hama benefited from its merchants' ties to Aleppo during the peak of the latter's prosperity in the seventeenth century. When the fortunes of Aleppo and northern Syria declined, in relative terms, during the eighteenth century, Hama became linked to new centers of regional wealth and power in Damascus.[27]

Until 1724–1725 the district of Hama was administratively subordinate to the littoral province of Tripoli, but afterwards it was part of the province of Damascus.[28] Hama served as a stopping point on the route to the Hijaz for pilgrims from Anatolia and northern Syria, and its transfer to Damascus in the eighteenth century reflected the increasing responsibility given to the governor (*wali*) of Damascus for the security of the Syrian pilgrimage caravan to Mecca.[29] The attachment of Hama to Damascus gave the latter's governors direct access

---

26 Urban prosperity within the Ottoman framework is discussed in André Raymond, *Grandes villes arabes à l'époque ottomane* (Paris, 1985), 54–66.

27 On the relative decline of Aleppo and northern Syria, see Abdel Nour, *Introduction*, 65–84; and Masters, *Origins*, 30–33.

28 Constantin François Volney, *Travels through Syria and Egypt*, 2nd ed., 2 vols. (London, 1788), 2:297; 'Abd al-Wadud Muhammad Yusuf [Barghuth], "Tarikh Hamah fi al-qarn al-thamin 'ashar," mimeo, n.d.,18.

29 Abdul-Karim Rafeq, *The Province of Damascus 1723-1783* (Beirut, 1966), 58-59; 'Abd al-Wadud Muhammad Yusuf Barghuth, "Liwa' Hamah fi al-qarn as-sadis 'ashar: nizam al-hukm wa-bunyat al-mujtama' min sijillat al-mahkama al-shar'iyya bi-Hamah" (M.A. thesis, 'Ayn Shams University, 1970), 168, 173.

to Hama's grain resources, needed not only to supply the provincial capital but also to provision the pilgrimage caravan.[30] The chief Ottoman official in Hama was the district governor (*mutasallim*). Consistent with a wider pattern in Syria, *mutasallims* of Hama came from the Ottoman military class and held titles of agha or bey. The *mutasallim* received assistance from a retinue of military and fiscal officers. Letters of appointment for Hama's *mutasallims* emphasized their police and tax duties, including protection of the pilgrimage caravan and the prompt and scrupulous remission of taxes.[31]

During the eighteenth and nineteenth centuries Syria and the rest of the Ottoman Empire were gradually and unevenly integrated into a Eurocentric world economy. In the nineteenth century the Ottoman state itself took on a new form through bureaucratization and the curbing of local autonomies, the better to administer its far-flung domains systematically in keeping with the demands of modern statehood within the emerging international system.[32] Hama was caught up in these currents, and by the early twentieth century the regional context in which its society and economy were embedded had significantly altered. Paradoxically, however, Hama had also by the twentieth century acquired its reputation as a 'traditional' and 'conservative' locality. Its social and economic life from the eighteenth to early twentieth centuries was indeed marked by important continuities. Nevertheless, some of what appeared 'traditional' in early twentieth-century Hama was of recent provenance and signaled the new circumstances of the nineteenth and twentieth centuries.

---

30 Abdel Nour, *Introduction*, 242–243.

31 Law Court Registers (LCR) of Hama 46:79, doc. 173, 5 Jumada II 1203/ 3 March 1798; 46:168, doc. 355, 14 Jumada I 1208/ 18 Dec. 1793.

32 Roger Owen, *The Middle East in the World Economy* (New York, 1981), *passim*; Donald Quataert, "The Age of Reforms, 1812–1914," in *An Economic and Social History of the Ottoman Empire*, ed. Halil Inalcik and Donald Quataert (Cambridge, 1994), 762.

Chapter Two: Families and Family Values

From at least the Middle Ages onward, political power in the towns and cities of the Arab East was mediated through local notables. Such intermediaries were cultivated by the mostly Turkic-speaking military dynasties of Mamluks and later of Ottomans. Inasmuch as these rulers defined themselves as defenders of Islam or of the Muslim holy places in the Hijaz, they sought allies from among the local Arabic-speaking 'ulama' ('learned men'), including many who established lineages characterized by their religious and legal learning and scholarship. Other allies and intermediaries were local military families, some of whom founded dynasties of their own. (The local Ayyubids who governed Hama under Mamluk auspices till the middle of the fourteenth century are an early example.) By the Ottoman period such intermediaries – collectively known as *a'yan* – were part and parcel of the system of government. At times of central government retrenchment or distraction, these *a'yan* enjoyed wider scope for the pursuit of their local and regional ambitions within the Ottoman framework. During periods of centralized assertion or reassertion, *a'yan* would more closely resemble 'servants of the state.' But even though the fortunes of particular military families rose and fell according to circumstances, the phenomenon of power intermediaries was remarkably enduring. In the pre-modern era of household-based political power, *a'yan* as a group became well-nigh indispensable to the functioning of the Ottoman state.

The category of *a'yan* is contested, with some historians preferring to use the term more narrowly than it has been defined here. Yet the word usefully conveys the intermediary function that these individuals and families fulfilled. We will, however, disaggregate the *a'yan* according to a distinction drawn by Julia Clancy-Smith between 'elites' and 'notables' in the context of Ottoman North Africa. Her differentiation emphasizes elites' and notables' respective bases of power and authority. Elites, she writes,

> drew some, although not all, of their political authority from relationships with the state – either contesting it or supporting it – or both [...]. Religious notables on the other hand, tapped deep into other sources – sharifian descent, special piety, erudition, charity – the attributes demanded of the holy person [...]. They [...] wielded sociospiritual and moral authority [...].[1]

Clancy-Smith acknowledges that elite and notable bases of authority often were intertwined, but the basic distinction between people of military and scholarly/religious status is relevant to the social structure of Ottoman towns including Hama.[2]

Hama's Upper-Class Families

In the eighteenth century three upper-class families dominated Hama's society. One was an elite family of military newcomers, the ʻAzms. The others were the Kaylanis and the ʻAlwanis, notable families with traditions of Islamic learning and religious leadership whose prominence in Hama went back many generations. In addition there were a few families of lesser notables, the most significant of whom were the Sharabis and the Hawranis. Most eighteenth-century notables, whether of the greater or lesser kind, were *ashraf* or formally recognized descendants of the Prophet Muhammad. The embodiment of *ashraf* notables' status and position was a mosque or Sufi lodge (*zawiya*) or both, associated with and named after one or another ancestor. Notable families tended to live in the quarters or neighborhoods where their ancestors' mosques or lodges were built. The social and religious prestige of the *ashraf* notable families was buttressed by their control of endowments that supported mosques, lodges, and benefactors' descendants. In this respect Hama was a microcosm of Damascus and Aleppo, and similar relationships are evident in smaller centers such

---

1 Julia A. Clancy-Smith, *Rebel and Saint: Muslim Notables, Populist Protest, Colonial Encounters (Algeria and Tunisia, 1800–1904)* (Berkeley, 1994), 269–270, n. 4.

2 Cf. Douwes, *Ottomans in Syria*, 63–66.

as Homs.[3] The influence of *ashraf* notable families in Hama is representative of a pattern that prevailed in the towns and cities of the Syrian interior.

The Kaylanis were a leading *ashraf* family of the eighteenth century. Of all Hama's *ashraf* they were the most successful in maintaining their predominance across the nineteenth and into the early twentieth centuries. Hama's Kaylanis were one branch of a lineage that went back to 'Abd al-Qadir al-Jilani of Baghdad (d. 1166), eponymous founder of the Qadiriyya Sufi order. His descendants were hereditary shaykhs of the order, which had established itself in Syria well before the Ottoman conquest.[4] However, the first Kaylani to leave a demonstrable imprint on Hama, Ibrahim, lived in the seventeenth century. He built a mosque on the right bank of the Orontes just downstream from a sharp, nearly right-angle bend in the river. Luxurious residences belonging to the Kaylani family were built nearby, and this section of al-Hadir became the locus of the Kaylani family's presence in Hama.[5] Since the fourteenth century a bridge, originally known as Jisr al-Afdal and later as Jisr al-Shaykh, had linked al-Hadir to the precincts of the twelfth-century Nur al-Din mosque on the left bank.[6] In the eighteenth century these districts of al-Hadir were called al-'Aqiba bi-al-Hadir and Qasabat al-Hadir, the 'casbah' of al-Hadir; but the environs of the Qadiriyya lodge and Kaylani mosques also came to be known as al-Kaylaniyya,[7] reflecting the decisive imprint that the Kaylanis had left on the neighborhood.

In addition to their hereditary leadership of the Qadiriyya Sufis,[8] the most pre-eminent Kaylanis were identified with the Ottoman-patronized Hanafi school of Islamic law. Kaylanis held many of the

3 Schilcher, *Families in Politics*, 194–207; Meriwether, *Kin Who Count*, 178–185; al-Zahrawi, *Usur Hims*, 3:63–64, 99, 110, 112–114.

4 EI, 2nd ed., s.v. "Kâdiriyya" by D. S. Margoliouth.

5 LCR Hama 46:253–254, doc. 542, 25 Dhu al-Qa'da 1211/ 22 May 1797.

6 EI, 2nd ed., s.v. "Hamât"; al-Sabuni, *Tarikh Hamah*, 97.

7 LCR Hama 46:151, doc 314, 29 Safar 1208/ 6 Oct. 1793; 46:178, doc. 375, 20 Jumada II 1208/ 23 Jan. 1794; *Hamah: Ma'sat al-'Asr* ([Lebanon], 1983), 50.

8 Cf. al-Nabulsi, *al-Haqiqa wa-al-Majaz*, 48–49; al-Sabuni, *Tarikh Hamah*, 173–174; LCR Hama 42:294, doc. 597, *awakhir* Shawwal 1140/ 8 June 1728 & 53:267, 9 Shawwal 1268/ 27 July 1852.

plum jobs in the religious and judicial hierarchy of eighteenth-century Hama. In the 1730s, 1770s and early 1790s they were counted among Hama's Hanafi muftis (jurisconsults).[9] For most of the 1790s a Kaylani also held the position of *naqib* or head of Hama's *ashraf*.[10] At the end of the eighteenth century Ibrahim Efendi al-Kaylani, a former mufti, had become Hama's deputy judge ('deputy' to the Ottoman-appointed judge in Damascus; in effect, therefore, Hama's Islamic law-court judge).[11] The appointment of Kaylanis to the top three positions in Hama's religious and judicial hierarchy during the 1790s – *naqib*, mufti, and deputy judge – testifies to the consolidation of the family's remarkable local prominence and it set the pattern for the following century.

Another important family of *ashraf* were the 'Alwanis. They were an old urban family whose presence in Hama antedated the Ottoman conquest. They traced the prominence of their lineage to a native son, al-Shaykh 'Alwan (d. 1529). He was a scholar who had established a mosque and Shadhiliyya Sufi lodge in al-'Alaylat quarter on the Suq side of the river (the left bank), where he had lived and worked.[12] Subsequent generations of 'Alwanis continued to live in and identify with al-'Alaylat,[13] and to serve as shaykhs of their ancestor's Sufi lodge and as custodians of his mosque.[14] Like the

9 Muhammad Hasan Efendi al-Kaylani, mufti in 1733; 'Ali Efendi al-Kaylani in the 1770s; Ibrahim Efendi al-Kaylani from 1790 to 1793, if not later. LCR Hama 42:394, doc. 790, 8 Dhu al-Hijja 1145/ 22 May 1733; 46:152, doc. 316, 5 Rabi' I 1208/ 11 Oct. 1793; 46:173, doc. 363, 10 Rabi' I 1207/ 26 Oct. 1792; Yusuf [Barghuth], "Tarikh Hamah," 41.

10 'Abd al-Razzaq Efendi al-Kaylani. LCR Hama 46:173, doc. 363, 10 Rabi' I 1207/ 26 Oct. 1792; 46:253–254, doc. 542, 25 Dhu al-Qa'da 1211/ 22 May 1797; 46:313, doc. 600, 6 Safar 1214/ 10 July 1799.

11 LCR Hama 46:316, doc. 602, 23 Safar 1214/ 27 July 1799.

12 al-Sabuni, *Tarikh Hamah*, 160–161; reference to al-Shaykh 'Alwan's mosque in LCR Hama 42:370, doc. 751, *awa'il* Rabi' I 1145/ 22 Aug. 1732.

13 LCR Hama 42:397–400, *muntasif* Muharram 1146/ 28 June 1733; 46:205a, doc. 466 [pt. 2], *awakhir* Jumada II 1209/ 21 Jan. 1795; 46:349–350, doc. 636, 21 Jumada II 1213/ 5 Dec. 1798.

14 E.g. the appointment of the former mufti al-Shaykh Ahmad Efendi to the headship of the 'Alwani lodge in LCR Hama 46:140, doc. 286, 15 Dhu al-

majority of urban Syrian Muslims, ‘Alwanis were affiliated with the Shafi‘i school of Islamic law and in the 1730s the Shafi‘i mufti of Hama was Muhi al-Din al-‘Alwani.[15] Later in the century, names of ‘Alwanis also appear on the roster of Hanafi muftis. Such legal diversification indicates a politic flexibility on the part of various ‘Alwani family members with respect to their law-school affiliations.[16]

Two other *ashraf* families of some importance were the Sharabis and the Hawranis. Although not in the same league of notability as the Kaylanis and ‘Alwanis (they were not, for instance, associated with the positions of deputy judge, *naqib*, or mufti), the Sharabis and Hawranis nevertheless shared some of the attributes of the more prominent *ashraf* families. Both established themselves in Hama in the mid- to late seventeenth century. The Sharabis traced their position in Hama to al-Shaykh Yusuf of the Sa‘diyya Sufis, who built the Sa‘diyya lodge in the left bank neighborhood of al-Safsafa.[17] The Hawranis' notable ancestor was al-Shaykh ‘Uthman of the Rifa‘iyya Sufis, who had settled in Hama from the Hawran region south of Damascus after the Ottoman conquest and built a Rifa‘iyya lodge in another left bank quarter, a portion of which subsequently became eponymously known as al-Hawarina after his family. As was common with holy men, al-Shaykh ‘Uthman was buried at the *zawiya* and his tomb became a locus of pilgrimage.[18] Both the Sa‘diyya and Rifa‘iyya orders were plebian in character, popular among the middle and lower social strata but reputedly viewed with suspicion by more orthodox jurists and Sufis.[19] The Sharabis' and Hawranis' status as *ashraf* and their hereditary links to specific neighborhoods and Sufi orders

---

Qa‘da 1207/ 24 June 1793; LCR Hama 46:127–128, doc. 265, 13 Jumada II 1206/ 7 Feb. 1792.

15 LCR Hama 42:404, doc. 803, *awakhir* Rabi‘ II 1146/ 9 Oct. 1733.

16 Ahmad Efendi al-‘Alwani in the 1770s and Amin Efendi al-‘Alwani in the 1780s. Yusuf [Barghuth], "Tarikh Hamah," 41.

17 LCR Hama 42:410, doc. 815, *awa'il* Dhu al-Qa‘da 1146/ 19 April 1734.

18 The quarter was Taht al-Shajara, part of which retained its original appellation. LCR Hama 42:410, doc. 815, *awa'il* Dhu al-Qa‘da 1146/ 19 April 1734; al-Sabuni, *Tarikh Hamah*, 69 n. 1, 100 n. 8.

19 EI, 2nd ed., s.v. "Rifâ‘iyya" by C. E. Bosworth; "Sa‘diyya" by Barbara von Schlegell.

assured them a role in the religious, judicial and political life of Hama. During the eighteenth century they represented the people of their neighborhoods to Ottoman officials, and in tandem with other notables (including ‘Alwanis and Kaylanis) they negotiated matters of public concern, particularly the payment of taxes.[20]

The establishment or consolidation of Sufi-linked notable families in Hama during the sixteenth and seventeenth centuries is a noteworthy development. Sufi Islam was a highly personalized form of religion, whose adherents followed the particular means or method (*tariqa*) to spirituality as defined by a founding holy man or saint. Selected students and disciples of the founder could inherit this authority and pass it along to their own followers in turn. Sufi spiritual genealogies extended from the present generation of devotees to their teachers and to their teachers' teachers, going all the way back to the founder of a particular order. As the Hama examples well illustrate, a strong hereditary element was characteristic of Sufi leadership.

The extension (or heightened visibility) of Sufism in the Ottoman Arab lands was a general phenomenon in the Ottoman period. For example, the presence of the Sa‘diyya Sufi order in Homs is attributed to a Sa‘di shaykh who built a *zawiya* there in 1618.[21] Sufi orders became salient features in Jerusalem's religious and social life at roughly the same time – i.e. the seventeenth century.[22] Sufi affiliations created horizontal ties among confreres across distances, and vertical ties within neighborhoods through the rites associated with visits to Sufi *zawiyas* and saints' tombs. Hence Sufism was an important part of the consolidation or assertion of the authority of notable families. Sufism may also have served to create links between elite and notable families, as apparently occurred in seventeenth-century Jerusalem.[23] In this respect, too, Hama can be regarded as a

---

20 LCR Hama 42:323, doc. 652, 12 Ramadan 1144/ 9 March 1732; 42:404, doc. 803, *awakhir* Rabi‘ II 1146/ 9 Oct. 1733.

21 al-Zahrawi, *Usur Hims*, 3:43.

22 Ze'evi, *Ottoman Century*, 68–76.

23 Ibid. Cf. Ruth Michal Roded, "Tradition and Change in Syria during the Last Decades of Ottoman Rule: The Urban Elite of Damascus, Aleppo, Homs and Hama, 1876–1918" (Ph.D. dissertation, University of Denver, 1984), 237–242.

microcosm of urban Syria in the middle period of Ottoman rule. For most people of Syria, religion was less a set of doctrinal abstractions and theological arguments than an integral part of social identity. People related to their beliefs by means of personal relationships: to pilgrimage sites, to saintly lineages and to local holy men, generalizations that are applicable to Muslims, Christians and Jews alike in the Ottoman-Arab regions. The Muslim notable families of Hama and elsewhere drew on an array of cultural resources – including popular religious authority – to buttress their claims to urban leadership.

The Kaylanis and ‘Alwanis were Ottoman Hama's most successful *ashraf* families. This success is measured by the length of time – over one century – that members of these families held prominent posts in Hama's religious and civil administrations. Up to the eighteenth century the leading members of the ‘Alwani family may have wielded more local influence than did their Kaylani counterparts. During that century the office of *naqib al-ashraf* was more frequently filled by an ‘Alwani than by a Kaylani.[24] By the 1790s at the latest, however, Kaylanis had surpassed ‘Alwanis in their occupancy of religious and judicial offices. In the mid-nineteenth century, members of the Kaylani family concurrently held the offices of mufti, *naqib*, and deputy judge, as well as continuing to exercise hereditary leadership of the Qadiriyya Sufi order.[25] The Kaylanis' monopolization of religious-judicial posts signified the consolidation of their position as Hama's pre-eminent family of *ashraf*, the only *ashraf* who

---

24 ‘Abd al-Mu‘ti al-‘Alwani in the 1730s; Mustafa al-‘Alwani in the third quarter of the century. LCR Hama 42:386, doc. 770, *awasit* Shawwal 1145/ 31 March 1733; al-Sabuni, *Tarikh Hamah*, 167. Douwes's generalization about the greater prominence of the Kaylanis vis-à-vis the ‘Alwanis is correct but mainly for the later part of the eighteenth century onward. *Ottomans in Syria*, 72.

25 The *naqib* was Muhammad Hasan Efendi al-Kaylani, the mufti was Muhammad Makram Efendi al-Kaylani, the shaykh of the Qadiriyya Sufis was Muhammad ‘Ali Efendi, and the judge was ‘Abd al-Qadir Efendi al-Kaylani (his immediate predecessor was Muhammad Abu al-Futuh Efendi al-Kaylani). LCR Hama 53:133, 25 Jumada I 1267/ 28 March 1851; 53:142, 1 Dhu al-Hijja 1267/ 27 Sept. 1851; 53:156, 24 Dhu al-Hijja 1267/ 20 Oct. 1851; 53:158–159, *ghayat* Dhu al-Hijja 1267/ 26 Oct. 1851; 53:197, 1 Rabi‘ I 1268/ 25 Dec. 1851; 53:267, 9 Shawwal 1268/ 27 July 1852.

numbered among the select group of Hama's large landed proprietors in the final Ottoman decades. The 'Alwanis, despite their relative decline in the nineteenth century, nevertheless continued to be counted among Hama's notables. The membership of Hama's advisory council in the mid-nineteenth century is evidence of this; out of the ten or so individuals on this new institution in 1851, four were *ashraf*: al-Shaykh Mustafa al-'Alwani and three Kaylanis.[26]

Notable families of 'ulama' and *ashraf* were associated with the fields of religion and law. Their notability was recognized by the Ottoman state, but their sources of prestige (*ashraf* lineage, leadership of Sufi orders) were not entirely state derived. This autonomous social prestige distinguished the Kaylanis and 'Alwanis from Hama's leading elite family, the 'Azms, whose position flowed directly from their links to the Ottoman state. The 'Azms' earliest known ancestor, Ibrahim Bey, was an Ottoman soldier in the seventeenth century in the region of Ma'arrat al-Nu'man between Hama and Aleppo.[27] After serving as district governor of Homs, Hama and Ma'arra for seven years, Ibrahim's son Isma'il Bey al-'Azm (d. 1733) was promoted to pasha and became governor of Damascus in 1725.[28] In the decades that followed, descendants and relatives of these 'Azms continued to occupy a prominent place in Hama's society. The most illustrious of the 'Azms, As'ad b. Isma'il (d. 1757), served as district governor of Hama before becoming governor of Damascus. His brother, Ibrahim Pasha (d. 1746), served as governor of Tripoli, Hama's outlet to the Mediterranean. Both As'ad and Ibrahim forged enduring ties to Hama,[29] which served as an economic and agricultural hinterland to

---

26 The Ottoman government established these advisory councils in the 1840s as part of its Tanzimat administrative reform program. The Kaylani members were the Qadiriyya shaykh, the mufti, and the *naqib*. LCR Hama 53:158–159, *ghayat* Dhu al-Hijja 1267/ 26 Oct. 1851; 53:197, 1 Rabi' I 1268/ 25 Dec. 1851.

27 Rafeq, *Province*, 86–92.

28 Ibid. 94; see also Munir al-Khuri 'Isa As'ad, *Tarikh Hims* (Homs, 1984), 2:342–344.

29 LCR Hama 42:276, doc. 569, *awasit* Muharram 1140/ 2 Sept. 1727; 42:329, doc. 667, 22 Sha'ban 1144/ 19 Feb. 1732; 42:410, doc. 815, *awa'il* Dhu al-Qa'da 1146/ 19 April 1734.

Tripoli and Damascus supplying these cities with silk and grain, respectively.[30] Hama's political re-orientation in the direction of Damascus in the eighteenth century was reflected in and reinforced by the consolidation of the 'Azm family's political power in the first part of that century.

Even though the wider political fortunes of the 'Azms waned in the last quarter of the eighteenth century, the family's name nevertheless retained its luster in Hama. The 'Azms' elite status survived, as demonstrated by Husayn Bey al-'Azm's membership of Hama's advisory council in 1851.[31] The clan's rise to local prominence anticipated that of other Ottoman military families who entered the ranks of Hama's elite in the first decades of the nineteenth century. Like the 'Azms, these parvenu military families were of non-Arab origin, usually Kurdish or Turcoman: the Barazis, Tayfurs and Jijaklis (Shishaklis). The latter appeared as tax farmers in the Hama district in the late 1820s.[32] The Tayfurs came to prominence shortly afterward during the period of Egyptian rule in Syria (1831–40), when 'Abdallah Agha Tayfur served briefly as deputy governor of Hama.[33] They continued to serve the state after the Ottomans re-established their authority in 1840; like the 'Azms, the Tayfurs had a seat on Hama's council in 1851.[34] The Tayfurs, along with aghas of the Barazi and Jijakli families,[35] acquired villages and farmlands in the process of landed estate-formation that characterized the last decades of Ottoman rule in Syria.

---

30 LCR Hama 46:56, doc. 136, 9 Jumada II 1202/ 17 March 1788; 46:117, doc. 241, 12 Safar 1206/ 11 Oct. 1791.

31 LCR Hama 53:158–159, *ghayat* Dhu al-Hijja 1267/ 26 Oct. 1851.

32 Dick Douwes, "Justice and Oppression: Ottoman Rule in the Province of Damascus and the District of Hama, 1785–1841" (Ph.D. dissertation, Nijmegen University, 1994), 61; idem, *Ottomans in Syria*, 68–69.

33 Douwes, *Ottomans in Syria*, 199.

34 Muhammad Kanj [Genç] Agha al-Tayfur. LCR Hama 53:158–159, *ghayat* Dhu al-Hijja 1267/ 26 Oct. 1851.

35 Bakir Agha al-Barazi and Ahmad Agha al-Jijakli. LCR Hama 53:88, *awakhir* Dhu al-Hijja 1266/ 5 Nov. 1850; 53:284, 11 Dhu al-Qa'da 1268/ 27 Aug. 1852; see also Douwes, *Ottomans in Syria*, 174–175.

Military families' prominence in Hama during the nineteenth century also reflects broader Syrian trends. Military factions in and around Damascus and Homs established themselves as local power-brokers, and, eventually, as leaders of urban society. Like the 'Azms, Tayfurs and Barazis, these military families levered their access to the riches of rural surplus into institutionalized political leadership. Examples include the Durubis, Jundis and Suwaydans in Homs, and the 'Abids and Yusufs in Damascus.[36]

Not everyone with a notable name was equally regarded; some shone more brightly than others. Male *ashraf* whose professional lives remained closely tied to religious and judicial institutions were extolled more highly in legal documents than were their non-'ulama' relations.[37] Female *ashraf* (sing. *sayyida* or *sharifa*) could transmit *ashraf* status to their descendants, even when their husbands were not themselves *ashraf*.[38] In addition *sayyidas* (like their brothers and male cousins) could bask in the reflected glory of their fathers' or grand-fathers' reputations.[39] However, since the prestigious posts that established and maintained *ashraf* reputations were not open to women, female *ashraf* did not establish matrilineal lines of shaykhs, 'ulama', and muftis. Neither could all males of a notable line realistically expect employment in the religious and judicial fields. Consequently some patrilineal lines of *ashraf* became identified with commerce and trade rather than with religious and judicial learning and leadership.[40]

---

36 As'ad, *Tarikh Hims*, 2:371, 378, 399, 410, 412–413; al-Zahrawi, *Usur Hims*, 3:75–76; Roded, "Tradition and Change," 274–275, 279; Khoury, *Urban Notables*, 37–40.

37 For Kaylanis cf. LCR Hama 46:178, doc. 375, 20 Jumada II 1208/ 23 Jan. 1794; and 46:186, doc. 412 [pt. 1], 4 Rajab 1208/ 5 Feb. 1794. For 'Alwanis cf. LCR Hama 46:140, doc. 286, 15 Dhu al-Qa'da 1207/ 24 June 1793; 46:380, doc. 681, 4 Sha'ban 1214/ 2 Jan. 1800.

38 E.g. LCR Hama 42:386, doc. 770, *awasit* Shawwal 1145/ 31 March 1733.

39 E.g. the 'Alwani and Kaylani *sayyidas* in LCR Hama 46:178, doc. 376, 20 Jumada II 1208/ 5 Feb. 1794; 46: 178, doc. 376, 20 Jumada II 1208/ 23 Jan. 1794.

40 E.g. the shopowners 'Abd al-Wahid b. 'Abd al-Rahman al-Kaylani and his wife Fatima bint Bakir; and the cloth merchant Salih b. Ahmad al-'Alwani. LCR Hama 46:174, docs. 367–368, 8 Rabi' II 1208/ 13 Nov. 1793; 46:379–380, doc. 676, 4 Sha'ban 1214/ 2 Jan. 1800.

Similarly, not all sons of shaykhs and scholars followed in their fathers' footsteps.[41]

Leading notable and elite families, especially the Kaylanis and the 'Azms, drew on various sources of wealth. Notable family strategies for preserving and maintaining the material basis of a lineage included endogamous marriages and marriage alliances, and the establishment of family endowments. The 'Azms, for their part, translated their political influence into substantial urban and rural property holdings.

Prestigious lineages were linked to family endowments. The family endowment – *waqf dhurri* – was a widespread Ottoman institution that allowed a person to endow his or her freehold properties for the benefit of designated relatives and descendants. The founder managed an endowment during his or her lifetime; subsequently, administration was vested in 'worthy descendants' who were to ensure good management of the endowed properties and the distribution of their revenues among the designated beneficiaries.[42] The whole process was subject to the oversight of the Islamic law court.[43] Because eligible beneficiaries were restricted to designated relatives and descendants of the founder, lineage carried not only social importance (in terms of one's prestige or standing), but also determined a person's claim to the revenues of one or another family endowment. Endowments of notable *ashraf* families often mixed piety and family, designating some revenues for purposes such as the payment of Qur'an reciters and supplies of lamp oil at mosques or

---

41 E.g. the coffee-shop proprietor 'Abdallah b. al-Shaykh Ishaq al-Kaylani. LCR Hama 46:113, doc. 233, 1 Muharram 1206/ 31 Aug. 1791.

42 For an example, see the endowment deed (*waqfiyya*) of al-Sayyid 'Abdallah b. al-Shaykh Sulayman al-'Alwani. LCR Hama 42:397–400, doc. 795, *muntasif* Muharram 1146/ 28 June 1733. A detailed treatment of this kind of endowment in the Syrian context is found in Randi Deguilhem-Schoem, "History of Waqf and Case-Studies from Damascus in Late Ottoman and French Mandatory Times" (Ph.D. dissertation, New York University, 1986).

43 E.g. judicial oversight of 'Alwani family *awqaf* in LCR Hama 46:381, doc. 682, 6 Sha'ban 1214/ 4 Jan. 1800.

lodges associated with the founder's family.[44] In this way notable lineages reproduced and renewed their association with particular religious or charitable institutions over a number of generations.

The principal *ashraf* family endowment in late eighteenth-century Hama was that of the scholar and businessman 'Abd al-Qadir al-Kaylani (d. 1744). He endowed property in both Hama and in villages outside of Damascus for the benefit of his descendants; he also established a Damascus branch of the family.[45] His endowment's properties in Hama included shops, orchards, a coffeehouse, a manufactory or workshop (*karkhana*), mills, a public bath, luxurious houses and simple dwellings.[46] The properties near Damascus were farmlands in the Ghuta (Damascus oasis) villages of Kafr Batna and Bayt Sawa. In the former village, 'Abd al-Qadir had endowed the farmland in association with his wife al-Sharifa Rahma bint 'Abd al-Rahman Efendi.[47] Other *ashraf* family endowments included those of 'Alwanis and Sharabis. The 'Alwani endowments consisted of market-garden lands located in the environs of Hama. By 1800 their administration had been joined to that of the endowment of one Ibrahim Chelebi, whose assets were located in Tripoli but administered from Hama. Ibrahim's 'Alwani descendants were responsible for all three of the endowments.[48] Possibly Ibrahim was a Tripoli

---

44 E.g. LCR Hama 42:397–400, doc. 795, *muntasif* Muharram 1146/ 28 June 1733; 42:410, doc. 815, *awa'il* Dhu al-Qa'da 1146/ 19 April 1734.

45 Schilcher, *Families in Politics*, 194.

46 LCR Hama 46:251–253, doc. 541, 13 Dhu al-Qa'da 1209/ 1 June 1795; 46:257, doc. 544, 25 Dhu al-Qa'da 1211/ 22 May 1797; 46: 253–254, doc. 542, 25 Dhu al-Qa'da 1211/ 22 May 1797. For a biographical sketch of 'Abd al-Qadir see Muhammad Khalil al-Muradi, *Silk al-Durar fi A'yan al-Qarn al-Thani 'Ashar* (Baghdad, 1874), 3:46–48. A comparably lavish endowment was established in 1820 by a subsequent Kaylani, 'Abd al-Qadir b. Ibrahim. Douwes, *Ottomans in Syria*, 73–74.

47 LCR Hama 46:256–257, doc. 543, 25 Dhu al-Qa'da 1211/ 22 May 1797; 46:257, doc. 544, 25 Dhu al-Qa'da 1211/ 22 May 1797.

48 LCR Hama 46:139, doc. 284, 15 Dhu al-Qa'da 1207/ 24 June 1793; 46:140, doc. 285, 15 Dhu al-Qa'da 1207/ 24 June 1793; 46:381, doc. 682, 6 Sha'ban 1214/ 4 Jan. 1800.

merchant who had married into the ‘Alwani family.[49] The Muhammad al-Sharabi endowment consisted of urban real estate, including shops and houses in the Sharabis' al-Safsafa quarter and nearby neighborhoods.[50]

By the late eighteenth century the benefits accruing to ‘Abd al-Qadir al-Kaylani's many descendants had become minutely subdivided and attenuated. Claimants generated legal documents specifying the rights and obligations of the various beneficiaries, but (in the words of one document relating to ‘Abd al-Qadir's endowment) ‘the multiplication of shares is leading the endowment to ruin and is destroying all of its traces.’[51] Clearly, then, it was not enough merely to be descended from the founder of a major endowment. Members of families like the Kaylanis and ‘Alwanis had constantly to find new opportunities to enhance and renew their own and their lineages' wealth. If they failed to do so they might, like the ‘Alwanis, suffer a relative decline in their fortunes even if they retained the cultural capital of their notable ancestry.

Notable families enjoyed basic security as property owners or as beneficiaries of family endowments, but the fortunes of military elites were not legally secure until the implementation of the Ottoman Tanzimat reforms in the nineteenth century. Prior to that time, military officials with the rank of agha, bey, or pasha were regarded as servants of the sultan. Upon their death or dismissal from office their properties were liable to confiscation (*musadara*) and accounting by representatives of the imperial treasury.[52] Even if an official acquired

---

49 In Iraq the sobriquet *chelebi* indicated an urban gentleman, often a merchant. In Syria, however, *chelebi* had a more general application. It signified a literate man who was not a religious shaykh or a member of the ‘ulama’ though he might be the son of such a person. Cf. Establet and Pascual, *Familles et fortunes*, 184; and Hanna Batatu, *The Old Social Classes and the Revolutionary Movements of Iraq: A Study of Iraq's Old Landed and Commercial Classes and its Communists, Ba‘thists, and Free Officers* (Princeton, 1978), 9.

50 LCR Hama 46:178, doc. 378, 17 Jumada I 1208/ 21 Dec. 1793; 46:190, doc. 426, 26 Rajab 1208/ 27 Feb. 1794; 46:192, doc. 430, 6 Sha‘ban 1208/ 9 March 1794.

51 LCR Hama 46: 253–254, doc. 542, 25 Dhu al-Qa‘da 1211/ 22 May 1797.

52 LCR Hama 46:131–132, docs. 272, 273, 24 Muharram 1207/ 11 Sept. 1792; 46:207–208, doc. 457–458 [pt. 1], *awasit* Dhu al-Hijja 1208/ 14 July 1794.

extensive properties during his term of office, he could not count on retaining them after his dismissal, or passing them along to his heirs. The widow of a pasha who wished to continue living in his house, for example, had to buy it back when the imperial treasury sold off her late husband's confiscated properties.[53] (Widows of notables or ordinary people, in contrast, normally inherited the conjugal home in whole or in part.)

Such insecurity of tenure helps to explain why elite dynasties were the exception rather than the rule prior to the nineteenth century. Whereas it is possible to trace notable dynasties of Kaylanis, 'Alwanis, Hawranis, and Sharabis over a number of generations, only one elite family enjoyed comparable longevity in Hama, namely the 'Azms. Their survival is attributable to the continuing need that the Ottomans had of them. As a locally based family with roots in central Syria, the 'Azms were useful to the Ottomans when strong and loyal local hands were required. However, when they died or fell from power, individual 'Azms had their properties confiscated in the same manner as happened to other military officials.[54] The vicissitudes of even a powerful dynastic family are demonstrated by the career of As'ad b. Isma'il al-'Azm. In 1732 a range of urban and rural properties were restored to As'ad Bey following his dismissal as

---

See also I. Metin Kunt, *The Sultan's Servants: The Transformation of Ottoman Provincial Government, 1550–1650* (New York, 1983), 32–33.

53 E.g. when 'A'isha Khanum, the widow of a certain Ibrahim Pasha, paid the treasury 3,500 piasters for her husband's large house and its effects; while at the same time the mufti, Ibrahim Efendi al-Kaylani, bought from the treasury a simple courtyard dwelling on the banks of the Orontes which had formerly belonged to the same Ibrahim Pasha. LCR Hama 46:167, docs. 353–354, 3 Jumada I 1208/ 7 Dec. 1793. This Ibrahim Pasha probably is not Ibrahim Pasha b. Isma'il Pasha al-'Azm. Although al-Sayyid Ibrahim (as he was known) died at Hama, many years separate his death (1746) from 'A'isha Khanum's purchase of her husband's house and effects. See 'Abd al-Qadir al-'Azm, *al-Usra al-'Azmiyya* (Damascus, 1960), 40.

54 E.g. the estate of Faris Bey al-'Azm. LCR Hama 46:207–208, doc. 457–458 [pt. 1], *awasit* Dhu al-Hijja 1208/ 14 July 1794. On the usefulness of the 'Azms to Istanbul, see Douwes, *Ottomans in Syria*, chap. 2.

district governor of Hama.[55] A few years later, in 1743, As'ad was promoted to the rank of pasha and became a successful governor of Damascus for 14 years. Yet in 1757 he was dismissed and executed, and the Ottoman state confiscated his property in response to the pecuniary needs of a newly enthroned sultan.[56] During his tenure in Damascus, As'ad Pasha established a family endowment which lent a certain stability to family fortunes, though it too was vulnerable to administrative and political pressures in ways that notable-family endowments were not.[57]

The opportunities for wealth accumulation that office holding provided are shown in enumerations of confiscated 'Azm fortunes. The properties of As'ad Bey, itemized in 1732, generated an annual net revenue of 2,462 piasters and included a marketplace (*qaysariyya*), a public bath, two water mills, and numerous orchards (*basatin*) in the vicinity of Hama.[58] To put the annual income figure of 2,462 piasters in perspective, compare it to the average price of a house or residence in Hama during the same period, namely 86.6 piasters.[59] The holdings of the late Faris Bey al-'Azm, enumerated in 1794, included livestock as well as properties in Hama, Homs, and the coastal towns of Tripoli, Latakia and Jabla that were appraised at 8,000 piasters.[60] During the same month, the properties of the late Muhammad Pasha al-'Azm, governor of Damascus for most of the years between 1771 and 1783, were appraised at 9,000 piasters.[61] (The average price of a residence in Hama during this period was 309.67 piasters.)[62] When oppor-

---

55 LCR Hama 42:328–329, docs. 665, 667, 22 Sha'ban 1144/ 19 February 1732 & *awasit* Shawwal 1144/ 11 April 1732.

56 al-'Azm, *al-Usra al-'Azmiyya*, 37–38; Douwes, *Ottomans in Syria*, 50–51.

57 A court document prepared at the end of the eighteenth century complains that the endowments and properties of the late As'ad Pasha had been subjected to 'onerous taxes.' LCR Hama 46:360, doc. 653, n.d. 1214/ 1799.

58 LCR Hama 42:328–329, doc. 665, *awasit* Shawwal 1144/ 11 April 1732.

59 Average price of all residences recorded in LCR Hama vol. 42.

60 LCR Hama 46:207–208, docs. 457–458 [pt. 1], *awasit* Dhu al-Hijja 1208/ 14 July 1794.

61 LCR Hama 46:206–207, doc. 454, 456, *awasit* Dhu al-Hijja 1208/ 14 July 1794.

62 Average price of all residences whose sales were recorded in LCR Hama vol. 46.

tunities for officials' personal aggrandizement were combined with legal security of property in the following century, it is little wonder that other military families in addition to the ʻAzms were catapulted into the ranks of Hama's elites. The only notables in the top rungs of Hama's landowning families on the eve of the First World War were the Kaylanis. All the other major landowners were elite families of military origin: the ʻAzms plus the arriviste families of Barazi and Tayfur.[63]

Elite and notable families practiced both endogamous and exogamous marriage, but on the basis of available evidence it is difficult to ascertain which type of marriage occurred more often. Because a bride joined her husband's family, endogamous marriage offered the advantage of keeping wealth and property within a family. Such was the case in marriages contracted within the Sharabi, ʻAlwani, Kaylani and ʻAzm families.[64] But exogamous marriages uniting families of similar social status also took place. For example, early in the eighteenth century the Hawrani and Sharabi families were linked by the union of a son of ʻUthman al-Hawrani, founder of the Rifaʻiyya Sufi lodge, and a daughter of Yusuf al-Sharabi, founder of the Saʻdiyya lodge.[65] Later one sees evidence of intermarriage and shared ancestry among Kaylanis and ʻAlwanis.[66] Kaylanis also intermarried with ʻAzms, including the union of Sulayman Pasha al-ʻAzm (d. 1743), Ismaʻil's brother who served as governor of Tripoli, with a woman of the Kaylani family whose descendants included ʻAzms and Kaylanis of Damascus.[67] In addition to intermarriage among families

---

63 Bell, *Syria*, 224.

64 LCR Hama 42:308, doc. 622, 20 Safar 1141/ 25 Sept. 1728; 42:397–400, doc. 795, *muntasif* Muharram 1146/ 28 June 1733; 46:142, doc. 288, 7 Dhu al-Qaʻda 1207/ 16 June 1793; 46:257, doc. 544, 25 Dhu al-Qaʻda 1211/ 22 May 1797. For the ʻAzms see their family tree in Schilcher, *Families in Politics*, 136 f.

65 LCR Hama 42:410, doc. 815, *awa'il* Dhu al-Qaʻda 1146/ 19 April 1734.

66 LCR Hama 46:313, doc. 600, 6 Safar 1214/ 10 July 1799; 46:379–80, doc. 676, 4 Shaʻban 1214/ 2 Jan. 1800; 53:38, 9 Rajab 1266/ 21 May 1850.

67 Schilcher, *Families in Politics*, 136 f., 194. Sulayman Pasha, the second ʻAzm governor of Damascus, married the daughter of a certain Yasin al-Qadiri (al-Kaylani), of whom little is known. For Damascene descendants of Sulayman

of similar social standing or background, some ‘Alwani men (at least) married women of non-Arab Ottoman or tribal background.[68] The relative weight of various considerations that went into such unions is impossible to ascertain at this historical distance. However, conjugal patterns were important for notable families because of marriage’s potential to strengthen or consolidate family solidarity (endogamous marriages), forge links to families of similar status, or build useful political or economic bridges to families with complementary resources (tribal and political ties). For instance, cooperation between members of the ‘Azm and Kaylani families was a characteristic of political life in Hama as late as the turn of the twentieth century.[69]

Elite and notable families lived in large extended households, with the palatial residences of ‘Azms, ‘Alwanis, and Kaylanis sheltering grandparents, their children and their grandchildren within expansive walled complexes.[70] In these circumstances the death of a patriarch produced a rearrangement of ownership shares and of living arrangements as married sons established their own independent households.[71] Yet the independent sons might live close to one another, as is evident in the example of three large adjoining Kaylani houses in al-Hadir.[72] When al-Shaykh Sharaf al-Din al-‘Alwani died in late 1793 or early 1794, his widow Fatima and her unmarried daughter Marwa sold their inheritance share of the lower part of the house to the Shaykh’s son ‘Abd al-Wahhab. Then they bought from

---

Pasha see LCR Damascus 697:190–191, doc. 142, 13 Rabi‘ II 1296/ 6 April 1879.

68 LCR Hama 42: 348, doc. 712, 20 Muharram 1145/ 13 July 1732.

69 M. Sükrü Hanioglu, “The Young Turks and the Arabs Before the Revolution of 1908,” in *The Origins of Arab Nationalism*, ed. Rashid Khalidi (New York, 1991), 40.

70 Such walled compounds were usually linked to elite and notable families. See LCR Hama 42:397–400, doc. 795, *muntasif* Muharram 1146/ 28 June 1733; 46:167, doc. 353, 3 Jumada I 1208/ 7 Dec. 1793; 46:207–208, doc. 457–458 [pt. 1], *awasit* Dhu al-Hijja 1208/ 14 July 1794; 46:254–254, doc. 542, 25 Dhu al-Qa‘da 1211/ 22 May 1797; 46:349–50, doc. 636, 21 Jumada II 1213/ 5 Dec. 1798; 53:91, *awakhir* Dhu al-Hijja 1266/ 5 Nov. 1850.

71 Meriwether, *Kin Who Count*, 79–95.

72 The houses are described in LCR 46:253–254, doc. 542, 25 Dhu al-Qa‘da 1211/ 22 May 1797.

‘Abd al-Wahhab his inheritance share of the upper part of the house. Thereafter the women owned and lived in the extensive ‘upper house’ (*al-dar al-fawqaniyya*), while their son/brother took possession of the ground-level rooms.[73] At times such a redivision of ownership preceded the formal division of a large house into two or more discrete units.[74]

Some if not all elite families had domestic slaves as part of their extended households.[75] Male slaves were entrusted with their masters’ business affairs,[76] and manumitted slaves remained part of an owner’s household.[77] The phenomenon of domestic slavery, and the inclusion of slaves in elite-family households, is one more example of the way in which Hama resembled other regions of the Ottoman-Arab world in the eighteenth and nineteenth centuries. The possession of slaves and the retention of manumitted slaves – whether within the household or as clients – was typical of elite social and political behavior. The presence of slaves and former slaves increased a household’s size, influence and resources.[78]

---

73 LCR Hama 46:178, docs. 375–376, 20 Jumada II 1208/ 23 Jan. 1794.

74 E.g. LCR Hama 46:160, doc. 337, 20 Rabi‘ I 1208/ 26 Oct. 1793; 46:227, doc. 503, 1 Rabi‘ II 1212/ 23 Sept. 1797; 53:59, 7 Shawwal 1266/ 16 Aug. 1850.

75 E.g. the inheritance of Amina bint Munla Ahmad, widow of Ahmad Agha al-Madiyub. Her estate included a black female slave named Mahbuba (‘Beloved’), whose value was appraised at 700 piasters. LCR Hama 53:91, *awakhir* Dhu al-Hijja 1266/ 5 Nov. 1850.

76 E.g. LCR Hama 42:394, doc. 790, 8 Dhu al-Hijja 1145/ 22 May 1733.

77 E.g. the manumitted female slave of Caucasian origin, Surunaz Qadin, who lived in the household of her former master, ‘Ali Yawur Bey, the district governor of Hama. Surunaz owned residential property in Istanbul, her ownership suggesting a significant degree of material support from ‘Ali Yawur. The document says only that she is his freed slave (*ma‘tuqa*), but it does not indicate whether he married her. Possibly she had been linked to him in concubinage before her manumission. LCR Hama 53:232, 11 Jumada II 1286/ 2 April 1852. On concubinage and marriage in elite Ottoman households see Mary Ann Fay, “Women and Waqf: Toward a Reconsideration of Women’s Place in the Mamluk Household,” *International Journal of Middle East Studies* 29 (1997):43–46.

78 Ehud R. Toledano, *The Ottoman Slave Trade and its Suppression, 1840–1890* (Princeton, 1982), 8.

Few names of elite-family women can be found at all in the Hama court registers.[79] The judicial sources' silence about these women raises questions about the extent to which their formal legal right to property was respected in eighteenth-century Hama. The fact that until the 1840s elite men's property was subject to confiscation and seizure by the imperial treasury may be one factor explaining the dearth of elite women in the court registers. When elite men died their property was the state's to dispose of and family members did not automatically inherit it. The only unambiguous documentary evidence that women of elite families in Hama could expect to inherit property comes from the mid-nineteenth century.[80] The scant mention of elite women in the Hama registers contrasts with that of notable-family women, whose names appear throughout the eighteenth century in the context of their purchase, sale, and inheritance of movable (and, to a lesser extent, immovable) properties, and as founders or beneficiaries of family endowments.[81]

---

79 In vol. 42 there are none; in vol. 46 there are just two: 'A'isha Khanum the wife of one Ibrahim Pasha, and Muhtab Qadin the wife of Faris Bey al-'Azm. (The Turkish titles *khanum* and *qadin* signify women of the elite, a status open to manumitted slaves also as evidenced in the preceding note.) In vol. 53 there is reference to two daughters of Muhammad Bey al-'Azm, but their names are not mentioned. LCR Hama 46: 167, doc. 353, 3 Jumada I 1208/ 7 Dec. 1793; 46:207–208, docs. 457–458 [pt. 1], *awasit* Dhu al-Hijja 1208/ 14 July 1794; 53:11, 22 Dhu al-Hijja 1265/ 8 Nov. 1849.

80 On his death in 1849 a dealer in cotton and livestock owed money to a great number of people including Muhammad Bey al-'Azm. Muhammad Bey had predeceased the cotton dealer, so the debt was owed instead to Muhammad Bey's heirs, two (unnamed) adult daughters. LCR Hama 53:11, 22 Dhu al-Hijja 1265/ 8 Nov. 1849. Similarly, the Hama widow of an agha was a joint heir (with her son) of her husband's house in Damascus. LCR Hama 53:37, 5 Rajab 1266/ 17 May 1850.

81 E.g. LCR Hama 42:348, doc. 712, 20 Muharram 1145/ 13 July 1732; 42:397–400, doc. 795, *muntasif* Muharram 1146/ 28 June 1733; 42:410, doc. 815, *awa'il* Dhu al-Qa'da 1146/ 19 April 1734; 46:113, doc. 233, 1 Muharram 1206/ 31 Aug. 1791; 46:142, doc. 288, 7 Dhu al-Qa'da 1207/ 16 June 1793; 46:178, doc. 375, 20 Jumada II 1208/ 23 Jan. 1794; 46:178, doc. 376, 20 Jumada II 1208/ 23 Jan. 1794; 46:257, doc. 544, 25 Dhu al-Qa'da 1211/ 22 May 1797; 46:379–380, doc. 676, 4 Sha'ban 1214/ 2 Jan. 1800.

Elite women's documentary invisibility cannot be generalized to characterize all women in Hama's society, a point that will be underscored when the roles and functions of lower-class families are discussed. The Hama pattern may not even be relevant to elite-family women in other Syrian centers. Early nineteenth-century, pre-Tanzimat judicial records from Damascus, for instance, include striking examples of elite-family women who controlled extensive properties and sources of income. These included women of the 'Azm family who endowed properties that they owned in the vicinity of Damascus.[82] Further afield, in eighteenth-century Egypt elite women of Mamluk households likewise had extensive commercial and property interests.[83]

One hypothesis to explain the absence of elite women from Hama's property records draws on the fact that elite families' wealth depended principally on their access to rural surplus and taxation. However, opportunities for Hama elites to acquire formal title (including inheritance rights) to land in their town's exposed hinterland was more limited than for their counterparts in Damascus or Egypt. In these latter places extensive regions of irrigated cultivation were characterized by deeply rooted traditions of private ownership. Consequently Hama's elites would have possessed fewer freehold (as opposed to tax-concession) properties, limiting elite women's legal access and title. This hypothesis is buttressed by Beshara Doumani's comparative study of family endowments of Tripoli and Nablus in the nineteenth century. Doumani has noticed that females were generally excluded from *waqf* benefits in Nablus, whereas they were included in Tripoli. He suggests that the divergent political economies – 'the differences in the key material base of propertied families' – between Nablus and Tripoli is the key to explaining this variation. Tripoli was surrounded by a lush green belt within which the property rights of

---

82 E.g. LCR Damascus 311:334–335, doc. 362, n.d. 1243/ 1827–1828; 312:49–50, doc. 152, 9 Muharram 1244/ 22 July 1828; 862, doc. 54, 17 Muharram 1306/ 23 Sept. 1888. The latter document refers to the endowment of Isma'il Pasha's daughter Zulaykha Khanum.

83 Afaf Lutfi al-Sayyid Marsot, *Women and Men in Late Eighteenth-Century Egypt* (Austin, 1995), chap. 3.

well-to-do-women were firmly established. In the garden-like surroundings of Tripoli, as in the Ghuta of Damascus, freehold and endowment properties were accessible to men and women with money. Moreover, legal rights to the property were firmly embedded in legal procedure, and management and exploitation of the property through hired foremen or agents was easy and practical. In contrast, access to the surplus of Nablus's hinterland required ongoing attention, surveillance, transacting, and alliance-building between Nabulsi elites and merchants, powerful rural chieftains, and rival political claimants, a situation that worked against the emergence of stable and enforceable urban property rights in rural areas.[84]

The relevance of this issue to the contrast between the visibility of Hama's notable women and the invisibility of their elite counterparts is that Hama's situation resembled aspects of both Tripoli and Nablus. Hama's rural surpluses were functionally divided between elite families whose military character allowed them to profit from fief-like tax farms some distance from Hama, and notable families whose large properties were concentrated in the Ghuta-like garden properties associated with the Orontes valley.

---

84 Beshara Doumani, "Endowing Family: Waqf, Property Devolution, and Gender in Greater Syria, 1800 to 1860," *Comparative Studies in Society and History* 40 (1998), 3-41, quote is on p. 40. Cf. James A. Reilly, "Rural Waqfs of Ottoman Damascus: Rights of Ownership, Possession and Tenancy," *Acta Orientalia* 51 (1990): 27–46; "Urban Hegemony in the Hinterland of Ottoman Damascus: Villages, Estates and Farms in the Nineteenth Century," in *Histoire économique et social de l'Empire ottoman et de la Turquie (1326–1960)*, ed. Daniel Panzac (Paris, 1995), 455–470; "Women in the Economic Life of Late-Ottoman Damascus," *Arabica* 42 (1995): 79–106.

Elite and notable families are relatively easy to identify and to document, because their properties and public activities left a substantial paper trail. But paradigms drawn from prominent families cannot automatically be applied to the majority of the population. For instance, we have seen that elites and notables drew income from their urban and rural properties, including family endowments. Reliance on income-producing property appears (in Hama, at least) to have enhanced or reinforced male authority and the importance of patrilineal bloodlines. But family endowments did not loom large in the lives of most people; commoners' relatively rare endowments usually were modest in scale.[85] Smaller endowments provided supplementary income, but they were not mainstays of subsistence. Nevertheless people coveted these endowment incomes, however slight. Some smaller endowments are known because of the judicial record left by individuals who vainly asserted their status as beneficiaries some generations after the endowment's establishment.[86]

When individuals of urban lower-class families owned immovable property, it usually was no more than the house or room in which they lived,[87] or (rarely) a house and a shop.[88] Here there was a significant difference between men and women. Only a small number of inheritance documents pertain to men who owned no immovable

85 The modest character of commoners' endowments is stated or implied in two documents, one of which speaks of an endowment that consists only of one room (*qa'a*) in a house; another of which seeks to trade commercially useless endowed land near a cemetery for half-interest in a shop used for pounding or beating cloth (*daqq al-qimash*). LCR Hama 46:189, doc. 423, 22 Rajab 1208/ 23 Feb. 1794; 53:288, 28 Dhu al-Qa'da 1268/ 11 Sept. 1852.

86 E.g. two cases nearly 100 years apart: LCR Hama 42:408, doc. 809, *ghurrat* Jumada II 1165/ 16 April 1752; 53:38, 11 Rajab 1266/ 23 May 1850.

87 Inheritance documents provide numerous examples from different decades. LCR Hama 42:335, doc. 684, *awasit* Dhu al-Qa'da 1144/ 10 May 1732; 46:240–241, doc. 524, 21 Jumada I 1211/ 22 Nov. 1796; 53:7, 25 Dhu al-Qa'da 1265/ 12 Oct. 1849.

88 LCR Hama 46:241–242, 20 Jumada I 1211/ 21 Nov. 1796.

property whatsoever.[89] In contrast, many women's estate inventories lacked immovable property. If a woman died before her husband did, she was unlikely to have owned the house in which she lived.[90] Nevertheless women did figure as owners of residential property, and their ownership was usually linked to family relationships. Often a woman inherited residential property after her husband's death as part of her delayed brideswealth[91] (*mu'akhkhar sadaq* – a sum owed to a woman from her husband's estate upon his death, or as compensation for a unilateral, male-initiated divorce). Alternatively, when a woman's husband was still living she might forgo her delayed brideswealth in return for title to a share of the family residence, a kind of 'anticipatory inheritance' that is especially noticeable in eighteenth-century documentation.[92] Women also actively acquired residential property through cash purchases, usually in collaboration with brothers and sisters, spouses, or parents. Thus one finds many examples of women buying house property from one or another parent, buying jointly with their husbands, or buying together with their sisters or brothers.[93] Bitter inheritance and legal disputes within

89 E.g. LCR 46:186, doc. 412 [pt. 2], 5 Rajab 1208/ 6 Feb. 1794; 53:24, 26 Rabi' I 1266/ 9 Feb. 1850. In the latter case the man was unmarried when he died.

90 A conclusion derived from a preponderance of women's estates in vols. 42, 46, and 53 of the Hama LCRs. For representative examples see LCR Hama 42:344, doc. 705, *ghurrat* Muharram 1145/ 24 June 1732; 46:270, doc. 565, 27 Rabi' II 1213/ 8 Oct. 1798; 53:20, 14 Rabi' I 1266/ 28 Jan. 1850.

91 Representative examples include LCR Hama 42:338, doc. 691, *awakhir* Dhu al-Qa'da 1144/ 25 May 1732; 46:149, doc. 312, 24 Safar 1208/ 1 Oct. 1793. By the mid-nineteenth century it was common for widows to receive delayed brideswealth in the form of cash, along with shares in jointly held residences which could then be consolidated through purchase and sale. See LCR Hama 53:52, 24 Ramadan 1266/ 3 Aug. 1850; 53:53, 27 Ramadan 1266/ 6 Aug. 1850; 53:61, 19 Shawwal 1266/ 28 Aug. 1850.

92 LCR Hama 42:273, doc. 564, n.d. Muharram 1140/ Aug.-Sept. 1727; 42:314, doc. 632, *awa'il* Jumada I 1141/ 3 Dec. 1728; 42:315, doc. 633, *awa'il* Jumada I 1141/ 3 Dec. 1728; 42:324, doc. 654, *awakhir* Ramadan 1144/ 27 March 1732; 46:146, doc. 298, 28 Muharram 1208/ 5 Sept. 1793; 46:188, doc. 420, 17 Rajab 1208/ 18 Feb. 1794.

93 E.g. LCR Hama 42:276, doc. 569, *awasit* Muharram 1140/ 2 Sept. 1727; 46:147, doc. 304, 3 Safar 1208/ 10 Sept. 1793; 46:149, doc. 309, 13 Safar 1208/ 20 Sept. 1793; 46:184, doc. 407, 29 Jumada II 1208/ 1 Feb. 1794; 53:4,

families pitted litigants against their own parents, siblings, children or in-laws over the ownership of house property.[94] The fundamental role that residential property played in ordinary families' financial status and security makes Hama once more a representative example of a wider Syrian urban pattern.[95]

Some better-off urbanites lived in comfortable houses capable of replicating, to a degree, the extended patrilineal household model of the aristocracy and the elite.[96] But other household models also existed. For instance, brothers might buy a house together and share the space among their respective families.[97] Many Hamawis lived in cramped quarters in close proximity to other, non-related families.[98] For people in such circumstances, the aristocratic model of the extended patrilineal family living within one large walled compound was unattainable. Instead they might find themselves in circumstances similar to those described by the French physician who in 1844 depicted the poor of Damascus as 'very numerous, poorly housed, poorly nourished, and hidden in quarters that are dark, humid, muddy

---

ghayat Shawwal 1265/ 17 Sept. 1849; 53:8, 28 Dhu al-Qa'da 1265/ 15 Oct. 1849; 53:29, 5 Jumada II 1266/ 18 April 1850.

94 E.g. LCR Hama 46:147, doc. 305, 8 Safar 1208/ 15 Sept. 1793; 46:183, doc. 403, 20 Jumada II 1208/ 23 Jan. 1794; 46:188, doc. 419, 17 Rajab 1208/ 18 Feb. 1794; 46:188, doc. 420, 17 Rajab 1208/ 18 Feb. 1794; 53:52, 24 Ramadan 1266/ 3 Aug. 1850; 53:53, 27 Ramadan 1266/ 6 Aug. 1850; 53:61, 19 Shawwal 1266/ 28 Aug. 1850. The significance of house property in Hama can be compared to the situation of Aleppo, suggesting a wider Ottoman pattern. Marcus, *Middle East*, 185.

95 Cf. Abraham Marcus, "Men, Women and Property: Dealers in Real Estate in 18th Century Aleppo," *Journal of the Economic and Social History of the Orient* 26 (1983): 137–163.

96 For instance, the houses in LCR Hama 46:151, doc. 315, 28 Safar 1208/ 5 Oct. 1793; 53:51, 21 Ramadan 1266/ 31 July 1850. Better-off (but not necessarily 'elite' or 'notable') urbanites also owned domestic slaves; see LCR Hama 46:208a, doc. 469, 21 Rajab 1209/ 11 Feb. 1795.

97 E.g. LCR Hama 42:408, doc. 808, *awasit* Jumada I 1146/ 24 Oct. 1733; 46:158, doc. 332, 2 Rabi' II 1208/ 7 Nov. 1793.

98 E.g. LCR Hama 42:312, doc. 631, *awa'il* Jumada I 1141/ 3 Dec. 1728; 46:147, doc. 304, 3 Safar 1208/ 10 Sept. 1793; 53:54, 27 Ramadan 1266/ 6 Aug. 1850.

and filthy.'[99] In such circumstances, the aristocratic model of the family was irrelevant to a majority of the Syrian urban population, except as a daydream.

Inheritance records show that early mortality in Ottoman Hama was commonplace. This represented another factor that limited the applicability of the patrilineal-aristocratic model. Children often predeceased their parents, and households were thrown into flux by the death of one or another spouse at an early age, an event which left widows or widowers responsible for bringing up of young children. Outbreaks of serious illness (including cholera and the plague) were a bane of existence during this period, further raising mortality and putting extra pressures on family structures.[100]

The centrality of family relationships extended into other spheres of economic life and activity besides ownership of residential property. Families of breadwinners who were injured or killed through accident or negligence demanded compensation. Examples include a middle-aged cotton porter struck by a runaway millstone that stonemasons were transporting through town; a woman trampled to death by a runaway horse; and a village youth killed by volleys of gunfire discharged during a wedding procession.[101]

Family ties were also an important means for financing business enterprises of middle- and lower-class people. Merchants and artisans tapped their relatives for loans and credit. For instance, nearly half of the estate of a carpenter who died while on the Mecca pilgrimage was pledged as a debt to his wife.[102] Over ten percent of a shopkeeper's

---

99 France, Archives du Ministère des relations extérieurs, Correspondance commerciale et consulaire (CC), Damas 1, Lautour, 22 Sept. 1844, p. 253.

100 E.g. LCR Hama 42:323, doc. 653, 12 Ramadan 1144/ 9 March 1732; 42:344, doc. 705, *ghurrat* Muharram 1145/ 24 June 1732; 46:156, doc. 328 [pt. 1], 22 Rabi' I 1208/ 28 Oct. 1793; 46:159, doc. 334 [pt. 1], *salkh* Rabi' I 1208/ 5 Nov. 1793; 46:193, doc. 436, 11 Sha'ban 1208/ 14 March 1794; 53:3, 9 Sha'ban 1265/ 30 June 1849; 53:5, *ghayat* Shawwal 1265/ 17 Sept. 1849; 53:17, 19 Safar 1266/ 4 Jan. 1850; 53:45, 14 Sha'ban 1266/ 25 June 1850. On public health in Hama see the critical comments of a local historian of the early twentieth century, Sabuni, in *Tarikh Hamah*, 116–118.

101 LCR Hama 46:160, doc. 338, 25 Rabi' II 1208/ 30 Nov. 1793; 53:56, 5 Shawwal 1266/ 14 Aug. 1850; 53:153, 27 Dhu al-Hijja 1267/ 23 Oct. 1851.

102 LCR Hama 46:240–241, doc. 524, 21 Jumada I 1211/ 22 Nov. 1796.

estate was owed as a debt to his mother.[103] Almost ten percent of the estate of a dry-goods seller was owed as a debt to his two daughters.[104] Nearly twenty percent of a furrier's inheritance was owed to a sister from whom he had borrowed.[105] Likewise, the major creditor of a thread merchant who died in 1793 was his wife; in fact his estate owed her more than it could pay.[106] Women's inheritances indicate that they could be creditors to a range of people, including but not limited to their relations. About one-third of the estate of al-Sayyida Diba bint Mustafa (d. 1793 or 1794) took the form of loans owed to her by five different men. One debtor was her husband, an agha, but his was not the largest amount due.[107] Another form of intra-spousal credit was a secured loan, such as the loan given by a wife to her husband, with the husband's ownership shares of their houses pledged as security.[108] In addition to being sources of credit, kin also were partners in farming enterprises, ownership of livestock, and some spheres of artisanal production.[109]

Thus the family – one's own household, as well as the obligations or entitlements or expectations of kin – served as a vital social and economic support network for middle- and lower-class people, notwithstanding the limited applicability of the aristocratic household model. The centrality of 'family values' – the value and utility of family and kin for social support, networking, and membership in society – is reflected in the low incidence of bachelorhood or spinsterhood. Moreover, widowed men and women, divorcées, and women deserted by their husbands sought remarriage.[110] The practice of polygyny, which in principle could help

---

103 LCR Hama 46:241-242, doc. 525, 20 Jumada I 1211/ 21 Nov. 1796.

104 LCR Hama 46:154, doc. 324, 19 Rabi' I 1208/ 25 Oct. 1793.

105 LCR Hama 53:25, 1 Safar 1266/ 17 Nov. 1849.

106 LCR Hama 46:148, doc. 306, 8 Safar 1208/ 15 Sept. 1793.

107 LCR Hama 46:187, doc. 416, 17 Jumada II 1208/ 20 Jan. 1794.

108 A type of transaction known as *bay' wafa'*. LCR Hama 53:47, 29 Sha'ban 1266/ 10 July 1850.

109 LCR Hama 53:8, 25 Dhu al-Qa'da 1265/ 12 Oct. 1849; 53:9, 5 Dhu al-Hijja 1265/ 22 Oct. 1849; 53:47, 29 Sha'ban 1266/ 10 July 1850.

110 E.g. LCR Hama 46:190–191, doc. 428, Sha'ban 1208/ March 1794; 46:216, doc. 483, 17 Shawwal 1209/ 7 May 1795; 46:244, doc. 530, 6 Rajab 1211/ 5

ensure that all eligible women got married, was in fact quite limited in practice. Monogamy was the norm. Few men had more than one wife at a time, and marriage to more than two women at a time was rarer still.[111] Hama's pattern of near-universal marriage, of remarriage after divorce or the death of a spouse, and the predominance of monogamy is similar to that noticed in Ottoman Damascus ca. 1700. The authors of the Damascus study, Colette Establet and Jean-Paul Pascual, in turn compared their results to those of Aleppo.[112] Considered in this context, the Hama material allows historians to generalize with increasing confidence about conjugal patterns in urban Syria during the Ottoman period in general, and the eighteenth century in particular.

Among elites and notables, families were political, social and economic units wherein pedigree significantly determined a person's access to resources. Notables' consciousness of their ancestry and of their aristocratic status is demonstrated by the persistence of their family names and institutions over two centuries or more. At the level of the middle and lower classes, family ties were crucial to providing people with the resources they needed to survive. Families were not only domestic units, but also were sources of credit and resource-sharing, and were loci of business partnerships. The other side of the coin was that familial interdependence also had the potential to create bitter conflicts over property and inheritance.

Women played subordinate roles within a male-dominated family structure, but they were by no means passive. Women of the lower classes particularly took part in household production and the extension of credit to relatives' business enterprises. Lower-class women did not hesitate to assert their rights in court when they believed that relatives or outsiders had treated them unjustly or

---

Jan. 1797; 53:62, 19 Shawwal 1266/ 28 Aug. 1850; 53:64, 28 Shawwal 1266/ 6 Sept. 1850.

111 Evidence for polygyny in the three volumes surveyed is limited to five documents: LCR Hama 42:338, doc. 691, *awakhir* Dhu al-Qa'da 1144/ 25 May 1732; 42:396, doc. 794, *awakhir* Dhu al-Hijja 1145/ 13 June 1733; 46:185, doc. 409, 2 Rajab 1208/ 3 Feb. 1794; 53:43, 27 Rajab 1266/ 8 June 1850; 53:47, 29 Sha'ban 1266/ 10 July 1850.

112 Establet and Pascual, *Familles et fortunes*, 50, 55–56.

illegally. If gender roles were relatively fixed in this period, women nonetheless used the norms, laws, and institutions at hand to defend or assert their rights to subsistence, inheritance, and property. The Islamic law court was a forum for such contests, particularly in the nineteenth century. Women's frequent use of the *shari'a* court from the eighteenth to mid-nineteenth centuries suggests that society's conflicts were increasingly subjected to formal adjudication. The growing case-load of the *shari'a* court in mid-nineteenth-century Hama was probably linked to the overall strengthening of bureaucratic authority in Ottoman Syria during the period of Ottoman reforms.

In most of these respects, the Hama evidence is consistent with that drawn from other Syrian/Ottoman centers at about the same time. The main differences in the status or roles of women are suggested by the low profile of elite women in Hama compared to those of Damascus, as well as the Hama sources' silence on craft licenses (see chapter four). The purchase and inheritance of these licenses formed noticeable parts of the Damascus and Aleppo records and gave women an ownership stake in manufacturing and commerce. More comparative work on family patterns in different Ottoman towns and regions will help to contextualize further the experiences of Hama's families.

Chapter Three: Social Networks

Twenty years ago historian Antoine Abdel-Nour asked how Arab cities in the Ottoman Empire actually functioned.[1] He was responding to an Orientalist model of 'the Islamic city' that emphasized or assumed its social fragmentation. Representing this view in the middle of the twentieth century, Gibb and Bowen wrote:

> [T]he Islamic city was not in any respect an organic unity. The social organization [...] was one of dislocated, self-contained and almost self-governing groups, subject only to the overriding authority of the temporal and spiritual powers [...].[2]

Abdel Nour interpreted the subsequent work of Ira Lapidus as a reiteration of the thesis that fragmentation characterized Muslim (and, by extension, Arab) cities in the pre-modern period.[3] Indeed, Lapidus's 'network model of Islamic society' articulated 'an image of society as a network of relationships between component groups rather than an image of society as an architectural or hierarchical structure.'[4] The urban population were divided into various groups defined by residence, occupation, or sect and – according to the network model – they constantly renegotiated their relationships with other groups through their shaykhs or group headmen.[5] Criticizing this characterization as 'schematic,' Abdel Nour responded by arguing that 'Arab cities' were more complex than allowed by Lapidus:

---

1 Abdel Nour, *Introduction*, xiv.

2 H. A. R. Gibb and Harold Bowen, *Islamic Society and the West: Islamic Society in the Eighteenth Century* (London, 1950), 277.

3 Abdel Nour, *Introduction*, 156.

4 Ira M. Lapidus, "Hierarchies and Networks: A Comparison of Chinese and Islamic Societies," in *Conflict and Control in Late Imperial China*, ed. Frederic Wakeman, Jr. and Carolyn Grant (Berkeley, 1975), 34–35.

5 Ibid. 37–38.

> Between the horizontal groupings of religious orders and craft corporations, and the vertical representation of shaykhs of quarters, chiefs of ethnic groups and of religious communities, there existed links and equilibriums which we only poorly glimpse, but which did not weigh less heavily on all of urban life and shaped it profoundly.[6]

Since Abdel Nour wrote these words, Lapidus has restated his social networks thesis in this manner: 'Invisible lines of reciprocal obligation ran through the whole of Muslim society, bonding disparate people and families together.'[7] Were he still alive, Abdel Nour might have appreciated this later reformulation and found it closer to his own.

Writing when he did, Abdel Nour could not clearly answer his own question about the inner workings of Syrian-Arab cities. However, the emergence of family history as a recognized field within Middle Eastern history offers new or additional tools for understanding the varieties of patronage and social networks in the Ottoman-Arab urban context. In Syrian cities, as we have seen, families of *ashraf* played a particularly important role. In many instances the status of the notable *ashraf* predated the Ottoman conquest. In other cases leading families acquired *ashraf* status as an accouterment of their power. The phenomenon of family-centered patrician power exercised through social networks allows the insertion of Arab or Middle Eastern cities into a wider discussion. Far from being unique to 'Muslim cities,' the relationship of patrician family power to social networks has a wide resonance, and may depend less on cultural ('Islamic') factors than on the dictates of urban life in preindustrial societies.[8] These general propositions can be tested or elaborated through an examination of the evidence from Hama, which in the Ottoman period was indeed characterized by interlocking and overlapping social networks. Upper-class families of elites and

---

6 Abdel Nour, *Introduction*, 156.

7 Ira M. Lapidus, "Muslim Cities as Plural Societies: The Politics of Intermediary Bodies," in *Urbanism in Islam: The Proceedings of the International Conference on Urbanism in Islam*, vol. 1 (Tokyo, 1989), 144.

8 Cf. Gideon Sjoberg, *The Preindustrial City: Past and Present* (New York, 1960), 321.

notables patronized these networks, which were defined by neighborhood, occupation, and confession.

Neighborhoods, Craft Corporations, and Communities

The previous chapter has argued that families and family ties were fundamental building blocks in Hama's society. Family ties intersected with other identities and occupations to make up the town's complex social fabric. These other loci of identity included the neighborhood or quarter, craft corporations, and religious or communal affiliations. Together they formed the social networks that defined and encompassed urban life in Syria during the Ottoman period.

Hama in the eighteenth century counted some 20–21 quarters (sing. *mahalla*) as summarized in Appendix 1. These may be compared to the list of 26 quarters drawn up in the early twentieth century by Hama's local historian al-Shaykh Ahmad al-Sabuni (Appendix 2). Data in Appendix 1 offer a rough guide to the relative wealth of the various quarters in the eighteenth century. It is noteworthy that the 1730s data rank at the top al-Hadir and al-'Alaylat, the respective abodes of the Kaylanis and 'Alwanis. Comparing the first three columns of Appendix 1 with the last column also demonstrates the flexibility or ductility of the definition of specific quarters, which could vary depending on time and circumstance.

Headmen (shaykhs) answered to officialdom on behalf of their quarters,[9] and petitioned the district governor on behalf of their constituents.[10] But the headman was not the be all and end all of quarter governance and representation; the quarter was a complex social organism, and within it were other foci of identification and representation as well. For instance, administration of the quarters was

9 LCR Hama 46:57, doc. 138, 3 Jumada II 1202/ 11 March 1788.

10 LCR Hama 42:323, doc. 652, 12 Ramadan 1144/ 9 March 1732.

vested in local residents identified as *ahl al-mahalla*, 'the people of the quarter.' When someone bought a residential property in Hama, the sales deed frequently specified that a fixed ground-rent (*hikr*) should be paid to *ahl al-mahalla*,[11] or alternatively to an endowment.[12] In one instance[13] the *hikr* was owed to an individual (Shaykh 'Abd al-Qadir al-Sharabi) apparently in his capacity as administrator of his great-grandfather's *waqf*.[14] At other times *hikr* was negotiated between homeowners and the 'elders' (*ikhtiyariyya*) of a quarter.[15] The *ahl al-mahalla* and *ikhtiyariyyat al-mahalla* shared fiscal and administrative functions with the quarter shaykhs. Sometimes they were linked to the major endowment of the quarter, underscoring the connection between notable families, their *awqaf* and their exercise of local leadership.

The law-court registers also refer to yet another type of urban representation: 'spokesmen' (*mutakallimin*) for the population.[16] Because the *mutakallimin* are referred to in the same breath as 'shaykhs of the quarters,' the shaykhs and *mutakallimin* might have been different people who served complementary functions. Thus various levels of representation and identification were at work in urban geography.

A single *mahalla* might be referred to by disparate names depending on circumstances. One vivid example is provided by al-Hadir. Typically the documents referred to the Kaylanis' neighborhood as '*mahallat* al-Hadir,'[17] but sometimes by the name of a sub-section such as '*mahallat* Qasabat al-Hadir'[18] or '*mahallat* al-'Aqiba bi-al-Hadir.'[19] Moreover, despite its frequent recurrence in judicial documents, the name al-Hadir does not appear in Appendix

11 E.g. LCR Hama 46:179, doc. 379, 17 Jumada I 1208/ 21 Dec. 1793.

12 E.g. LCR Hama 46:184, doc. 405, 5 Jumada II 1208/ 8 Jan. 1794.

13 LCR Hama 46:178, doc. 378, 17 Jumada I 1208/ 21 Dec. 1793.

14 LCR Hama 46:192, doc. 430, 6 Sha'ban 1208/ 9 March 1794.

15 LCR Hama 46:186, doc. 413, 5 Rajab 1208/ 6 Feb. 1794; 46:187, doc. 417 [pt. 1], 17 Jumada I 1208/ 21 Dec. 1793.

16 LCR Hama 46:57, doc. 138, 3 Jumada II 1202/ 11 March 1788.

17 E.g. LCR Hama 46:253–254, doc. 542, 25 Dhu al-Qa'da 1211/ 22 May 1797.

18 LCR Hama 46:151, doc. 314, 29 Safar 1208/ 6 Oct. 1793.

19 LCR Hama 46:178, doc. 375, 20 Jumada II 1208/ 23 Jan. 1794.

1's list of Hama's *mahallas* in 1800. Instead, al-Hadir's tax assessments were distributed among its sub-units including al-Zanbaqi wa-al-Jura. (Appendix 2 demonstrates that by the early twentieth century, the appellation al-Hadir had come to be applied to the entire right-bank section of Hama.) Other neighborhoods also were recognized or known by more than one name, especially when they were connected to ethnic or confessional identities. For instance, the 1800 list (Appendix 1) makes no mention of the 'districts' (sing. *hara*) of Christians or of Sakhana, yet both of these are mentioned around this same period in other contexts. The 'Christian district' (*harat* al-Nasara) was a part of *harat* or *mahallat* al-Madina, which adjoined the Great Mosque.[20] Moreover, *mahallat* al-Nasara is specifically mentioned in all three of the 1730s tax registers. The Sakhana quarter was named after people of desert origin – putatively from the oasis settlement of al-Sukhna – who specialized in trans-desert trade and in the provisioning of the annual pilgrimage caravan at the local government's behest.[21] Settlements of Sakhana were found in a number of other Syrian towns including Aleppo and Damascus, where they performed similar specialized economic functions. Those whom Hamawis, Damascene and Aleppines called Sakhana in fact hailed from any number of desert oases, including Palmyra, Qariyatayn, and the satellite oases of Sukhna as well as from Sukhna itself.[22] Located at the extreme northern edge of Hama on the right bank of the Orontes, al-Sakhana district was possibly subsumed in Appendix 1's

---

20 For *harat* al-Nasara see, e.g. LCR Hama 46:187, doc. 418, 20 Rajab 1208/ 21 Feb. 1794. For the identification of *harat* al-Nasara with *harat* al-Madina see 46:183, doc. 400, 15 Jumada II 1208/ 18 Jan. 1794. For a reference to *mahallat* al-Madina see 46:113, doc. 233, 1 Muharram 1206/ 31 Aug. 1791. On the location of the Great Mosque see al-Sabuni, *Tarikh Hamah*, 103. As a general rule, a quarter (*mahalla*) included within it one or more districts (sing. *hara*). However, in the instance just cited, *mahalla* and *hara* were used interchangeably. Therefore the distinction between them was not as clear in the eighteenth century as it became later in the era of the Ottoman administrative reforms. Cf. Abdel-Nour, *Introduction*, 158–60.

21 Yusuf [Barghuth], "Tarikh Hamah," 62.

22 Ahmad Wasfi Zakarayya, *Asha'ir al-Sham*, 2nd ed. (Damascus, 1983), 26.

fiscal list of 1800 under the heading al-Shamaliyya, 'the northern [district].'

The complexity of authority and representation in Hama's quarters is evocative of Damascus, whose extramural suburbs of the Midan and Salihiyya have been subjects of recently published studies. The Midan in the eighteenth and nineteenth centuries is characterized as being dominated by a small number of elite and notable families with complex and multi-stranded horizontal ties to each other, and who exercised authority through equally complex clientage networks.[23] A second recent study identifies persons who acted as 'notables' in nineteenth-century Salihiyya, yet who did not hold any administrative office. These quarter notables owed their reputations partly to their pedigrees, but also to their personal reputations for probity, good judgment, and dignified behavior.[24] Both Hama and Damascus corroborate Abdel Nour's contention that Syrian cities were characterized by complex yet poorly glimpsed interlocking social networks.[25]

Neighborhood-based social networks operated at different levels simultaneously: those of *mahalla*, of *hara*, and of ethnicity. Shaykhs and elders had overlapping spheres of authority, and at this historical distance from the eighteenth century one cannot be certain about the respective roles of shaykhs, *mutakallimin*, *ahl al-mahalla* and local notables in the unfolding of urban political life. The Christian and Sakhana districts highlight religion and ethnicity as significant elements of Hama's social networks. These identities mattered according to circumstance. A fiscal record dated 1800 designates Christians as a distinct group subject to special taxation, and records from both the eighteenth and nineteenth centuries designate groups of Turcomans, bedouins, and Kurds as tribal and ethnic collectivities with whom officials dealt.[26]

---

23 Marino, *Faubourg du Midan*, 315–348.

24 Miura, "Personal Networks."

25 Abdel Nour, *Introduction*, 156.

26 The exact reference to Christians in the fiscal document is *jama'at al-dhimmiyyin*, 'the group of *dhimmis*,' which in principle could have included Jews as well as Christians. But there is no evidence of a settled Jewish community in Hama during this period. LCR Hama 46:376, doc. 672, *awasit*

Confessional identity served both a social and psychological function. Whereas the Muslim majority could identify with the rituals, traditions, sites and families associated with specific Sufi orders, Christians found local identity in their churches and congregations. Confessional affiliation was also a resource for poor-relief and for charity.[27] Christians in Hama were overwhelmingly Orthodox. They were spared the debilitating schisms between Orthodox and Uniates that rocked Christians of Aleppo, where Uniate identity was connected to the established presence of trade and consular representatives from European Catholic countries.[28] Christians in Hama lived somewhat in the shadow of their co-religionists in Homs. The latter town was the seat of an Orthodox bishop, and one of Homs's churches was (and is) the proud custodian of the Virgin's waistband, a relic that attracted pilgrims and visitors. Moreover, since early Christian times a cult had developed around a local Homs saint.[29] The Christian churches of Hama boasted no comparable attractions.

Tribal and ethnic consciousness also served the social and psychological purpose of affiliation and belonging, reinforced by a division of labor that gave a utilitarian dimension to tribal and ethnic identities. Turcomans were communally identified with certain villages, and membership in such village communities meant, ipso facto, affiliation with Turcoman identity. Kurds were prominent among the paramilitary aghas, who controlled the provisioning of sheep and their wool to the Hama region by virtue of their ethnic and kinship ties to the hills and pastures of Anatolia. Local bedouins were relays in the trade between steppe and city. The aforementioned Sakhana were a Syrian-focused 'trading diaspora' who provisioned and organized

Ramadan 1214/ 10 Feb. 1800. The phrase for bedouins is *'ashayir* [*sic*] al-'Arab, 'Arab tribes,' and for Turcomans is al-Turkuman *al-iskan* ('settled Turcomans'?). LCR Hama 42:322, docs. 650–651, *awa'il* Sha'ban 1144/ 29 Jan. 1732; 46:105, doc. 206, 1 Rajab 1205/ 6 March 1791; 46:113, doc. 234, 22 Muharram 1206/ 21 Sept. 1791; 53:56, 7 Shawwal 1266/ 16 Aug. 1850; 53:79–80, 27 Dhu al-Qa'da 1266/ 4 Oct. 1850; 53:241, 17 Rajab 1268/ 7 May 1852.

27 Cf. Marcus, *Middle East on the Eve of Modernity*, 212–218.

28 Ibid. 47–48.

29 al-Zahrawi, *Usur Hims*, 2: 130–134.

caravans across the Syrian steppes and desert. Religious, tribal, and ethnic identities were not simply or merely a matter of real or fictitious 'blood ties,' or of primordialism run rampant. Rather, they were practical markers that helped to define people's functions and roles in a complex society not yet subjected to the disruptive and socially homogenizing forces of capitalism and industrialization.

With all of the varieties of their identities and social networks, Hama and its hinterland would seem to recall the metaphor of a 'social mosaic.' But this metaphor understates the overlapping and interwoven characteristics of Syria's social networks. The example of Hama demonstrates that these networks formed more of a complex tapestry than a mosaic. The confessionally mixed networks formed by craft corporations[30] and some urban neighborhoods[31] are cases in point, as are the unmediated commercial dealings between individual townspeople and bedouins.[32] The tapestry metaphor serves as a reminder that Hamawis, like other people, had a multiplicity of identities. They belonged to clusters of networks that placed demands on their loyalties and behavior depending on particular pressures and circumstances. Ottoman Hama was a society of intertwined social net-

---

30 E.g. the corporations (sing. *ta'ifa*) of merchants, apothecaries, and copper workers. LCR Hama 46:243, doc. 569, 8 Rajab 1211/ 7 Jan. 1797.

31 Demonstrated across the decades in, e.g. the following documents: LCR Hama 42:323, doc. 652, 12 Ramadan 1144/ 9 March 1732; 42:360, doc. 772, 25 Safar 1145/ 17 Aug. 1732; 46:174, doc. 366, 8 Rabi' II 1208/ 13 Nov. 1793; 46:186, doc. 413, 5 Rajab 1208/ 6 Feb. 1794; 53:50, 19 Ramadan 1266/ 29 July 1850.

32 E.g. Muhammad al-Hamad, 'the bedouin from the Iskandar Arabs,' who was a creditor to two beys and to an 'Alwani; the urbanite 'Izz al-Din b. al-Hajj A'rabi who was a creditor to a Bani Khalid bedouin; the wool dealer 'Abd al-Rahman al-Sawwaf who was a creditor to one 'Muhammad the Bedouin'; and the existence of a partnership between a bedouin and a man linked to Hama's dye trade. LCR Hama 46:154, doc. 321, 14 Rabi' I 1208/ 20 Oct. 1793; 46:165, doc. 348, 18 Jumada I 1208/ 22 Dec. 1793; 46:191, doc. 426 [pt. 1], 13 Jumada I 1208/ 17 Dec. 1793; 46:445–446, doc. 533 [pt. 1], 27 Rajab 1211/ 26 Jan. 1797.

works whose boundaries overlapped and blurred.[33] How Hamawis defined and understood their interests, the forms taken by political relationships, and the relationship of the latter to the social tapestry bring the discussion back to the 'elites' and 'notables,' leaders of local society who were recognized and dealt with as such by Ottoman officials.

Elites, Notables, and Social Networks

Craft corporations numbered in their ranks a significant proportion of Hama's productive population. The corporations were the most extensive type of urban social network to which elites were linked. They were fiscal and regulatory units that, *inter alia*, served the elite[34] through the provision of goods and services. At the same time, members of the elite patronized craft corporations by extending loans and credit and by granting tax deferrals.[35] The largest single purchaser of the craft corporations' goods and services was the district governor's headquarters, the serail.[36] On occasion these *mutasallims* mustered the craft corporations for marches and celebrations, such as the one marking the victory of Ottoman governor al-Jazzar over Napoleon Bonaparte at Acre in 1799.[37] Not just elites but also notables had close relations with craft corporations. For instance, in 1732 al-Shaykh 'Abd al-Razzaq Efendi al-Kaylani helped the bakers

---

33 Cf. the discussion of pre-colonial Bengal in Partha Chatterjee, *The Nation and its Fragments: Colonial and Postcolonial Histories* (Princeton, 1993), 221–223.

34 See, e.g. the organization of the butchers' tax farm in LCR Hama 46:237, doc. 519, n.d. Sha'ban 1210/ Feb.–March 1796.

35 LCR Hama 42:323, doc. 652, 12 Ramadan 1144/ 9 March 1732; 42:339, doc. 694, *awakhir* Dhu al-Hijja 1144/ 23 June 1732.

36 See, e.g. LCR Hama 46:52, doc. 123, 8 Muharram 1202/ 20 Oct. 1787; 46:177, doc. 373, n.d. Rajab 1208/ Feb.–Mar. 1794; 46:243, doc. 569, 8 Rajab 1211/ 7 Jan. 1797.

37 LCR Hama 46:276, doc. 567, n.d. 1213/ 1799.

(*khabbazin*) repay a debt to Mustafa Agha Badran Zadah al-Halabi, a debt which the *khabbazin* had incurred for wheat deliveries.[38] In the same period, the Shafi'i mufti Muhi al-Din al-'Alwani joined with the *naqib al-ashraf*, 'Abd al-Mu'ti al-'Alwani, and other shaykhs and *ashraf* from the Sharabi and Hawrani families to guarantee a debt (probably deferred taxes) owed to a certain Ibish Bey b. Ibrahim Pasha by the heads of the *suq* in general, and by the butchers and bakers in particular.[39] Thus notables acted as patrons of the craft corporations, offering their protection or at least serving as a buffer in the corporations' dealings with revenue-obsessed officials. The patronage of *ashraf* and shaykhs is indicative of close links between local religious figures and institutions (including Sufi orders) and craft corporations. This relationship has parallels with the situation of Damascus, whose craft corporations were tied to Sufism by leadership, ritual, and ceremony.[40]

Elites also associated themselves with merchants and traders. In part this relationship grew out of elites' (particularly *mutasallims'*) official responsibilities, notably overseeing and protecting the annual pilgrimage caravan to and from Mecca when it passed through Hama district.[41] The caravan had great commercial significance,[42] and supplying its needs enmeshed elites in the camel trade.[43] Hama's *mutasallims* also intervened in the eighteenth-century silk trade between Tripoli and Hama.[44] Merchants' prosperity depended to a degree on the kind of relationship that they had with the *mutasallim*

---

38 LCR Hama 42:339, doc. 694, *awakhir* Dhu al-Hijja 1144/ 23 June 1732.

39 LCR Hama 42:404, doc. 803, *awakhir* Rabi' II 1146/ 9 Oct. 1733.

40 R. D. McChesney (tr.), "Ilyas Qudsi on the Craft Organizations of Damascus in the Late Nineteenth Century," in *A Way Prepared: Essays on Islamic Culture in Honor of Richard Bayly Winder,* ed. Farhad Kazemi and R. D. McChesney (New York, 1988), 80–106 (*passim*); Schilcher, *Families in Politics*, 201–204.

41 LCR Hama 46:79–80, doc. 173, 5 Jumada II 1203/ 3 March 1789.

42 Yusuf [Barghuth], "Tarikh Hamah," 62–63; Abdul-Karim Rafeq, "Mazahir iqtisadiyya wa-ijtima'iyya min liwa' Hamah 942–943/ 1535-1536," *Dirasat Tarikhiyya* no. 31–32 (March-June 1989), 38.

43 LCR Hama 46:247, doc. 535, 2 Ramadan 1211/ 1 March 1797.

44 LCR Hama 46:117, doc. 241, 12 Safar 1206/ 11 Oct. 1791; 46:118, doc. 244, 15 Safar 1206/ 14 Oct. 1791.

and the local elites.[45] At one point the governor of Damascus owned a *qaysariyya* (covered market or caravansary)[46] in Hama that he had purchased from a local agha.[47] A member of the local administrative elite, A'rabi Agha al-Hatahit, bought six shops in Suq al-Mansuriyya in 1792, and he was promised ownership of any dwellings he might build in an adjoining vacant enclosure.[48] A'rabi Agha's possession of shops had the potential to create a proprietary or patronage relationship between him and any craft workers to whom he might let out the shops. At the same time, shop possession made him responsible to the administrators of the Kaylani *waqf* to which the land and shops ultimately belonged.

In addition to their association with craft corporations, trade and commerce, elites also extended their influence into the countryside where they were tax collectors and enforcers of government authority. *Mutasallims* and aghas were responsible for provisioning troops and towns with grain,[49] and so they also acted as grain merchants.[50] The line often was blurred between grain whose revenues were directed to the provincial treasury and grain whose revenues were pocketed by tax collectors and administrators in lieu of pay, or as a supplement to 'legitimate' income.[51] This form of institutionalized or routine corruption was common to other Ottoman provinces in the eighteenth century, and paradoxically it served to buttress local officials' ultimate loyalty to and dependence on the central government in Istanbul.[52] The associates of aghas and *mutasallims* in Hama's countryside included urban-based moneylenders and tax farmers who served as relays between the governor and district governors, on the one hand,

45 LCR Hama 46:259, doc. 546, 13 Sha'ban 1213/ 20 Jan. 1799.

46 On *qaysariyya* see Raymond, *Artisans*, 1:252–253.

47 LCR Hama 46:96–97, doc. 196, 3 Rabi' I 1204/ 21 Nov. 1789.

48 LCR Hama 46:126, docs. 260–263, 1 Jumada II 1206/ 26 Jan. 1792.

49 LCR Hama 46:56, doc. 136, 9 Jumada II 1202/ 17 March 1788; 46:226, doc. 502, 11 Muharram 1210/ 28 July 1795; 46:360, doc. 652, 28 Safar 1214/ 1 Aug. 1799.

50 As'ad, *Tarikh Hims*, 2:342.

51 See, e.g. LCR Hama 42:281, doc. 577, 23 Rabi' I 1140/ 8 Nov. 1727.

52 Douwes, *Ottomans in Syria*, 162–163.

and villagers and their representatives on the other.[53] Elites' fiscal privileges were sublet; in 1793, for instance, an agha and a Christian moneylender sublet from Turcoman elders (*ikhtiyariyya*) the latter's right to the taxes of Turcoman villages outside of Hama.[54] Elites' fiscal authority could resemble a de facto form of proprietorship, whereby a village was designated as being 'dependent upon' (*tabi'a ila*) a given agha.[55] In the pre-nineteenth-century Ottoman context, such 'dependence' referred to the agha's right to appropriate a village's taxed surplus. Therefore an agha's proprietorship of a village did not (yet) approach the theory and practice of private landownership, the full development and codification of which occurred in the next century. Rather, one sees here aghas acting as claimants to agricultural revenue, befitting their role in the Ottoman food chain that linked the big fish of Istanbul to the minnow-like peasants of the provinces.[56] Individuals of the elite amassed considerable fortunes in agriculture through ownership of cultivation rights and speculative advance purchases of crops (*daman*).[57] Some also owned significant herds of livestock, especially sheep.[58] Trade in livestock was especially identified with elites of Kurdish and Turcoman origin.[59]

Besides relying on military and administrative elites, the Ottomans also depended on local notables to solidify their rule. To the extent that notables, including those of the 'Alwani and Kaylani families, ameliorated the misdeeds of venal or unjust officials, they defended the interests of the community and added to their own professional and familial luster. An eighteenth-century chronicle from

53 LCR Hama 42:414, doc. 819, *awasit* Dhu al-Hijja 1146/ 19 May 1734; 46:160, doc. 339, 28 Rabi' II 1208/ 3 Dec. 1793.

54 LCR Hama 46:155, doc. 325, 21 Rabi' I 1208/ 27 Oct. 1793.

55 E.g. LCR Hama 46:144, doc. 292, 15 Muharram 1208/ 23 Aug. 1793.

56 Cf. Tosun Aricanli and Mara Thomas, "Sidestepping Capitalism: On the Ottoman Road to Elsewhere," *Journal of Historical Sociology* 7, no. 1 (March 1994), 27–29, 35–36.

57 E.g. the receipts of Faris Bey al-'Azm in LCR Hama 46:164, doc. 346, n.d. 1207–1208/ 1792–1794.

58 E.g. LCR Hama 46:66–68, doc. 161, 19 Dhu al-Qa'da 1202/ 21 Aug. 1788.

59 Rafeq, "Mazahir iqtisadiyya,"18; As'ad, *Tarikh Hims*, 2:332, 343.

Homs repeatedly demonstrates the succor that townspeople sought from their notables to defend them against injustice and hardship.[60] In Hama one sees notables' attempts to insert themselves as buffers between quarters and craft corporations, on the one hand, and tax-collecting officials on the other hand. Unlike most of the military-administrative elite, notables' authority had a moral component and did not depend exclusively on their appointment to offices. Highly regarded religious notables retained their moral authority even after dismissal or retirement from appointed positions, and some enjoyed reputations that extended beyond their home towns.[61] They used their cultural capital and religio-judicial positions to amass and consolidate material affluence, a virtuous circle (from their point of view) that further buttressed their positions as local notables and natural leaders of urban society. As Sufi shaykhs, jurisconsults, deputy judges and preachers, the leading lights of the Kaylani and 'Alwani families represented both popular religious devotion and the legal-scholarly vocation.

'Alwanis, Kaylanis, and lesser notables were administrators of charitable endowments including mosques and hospices.[62] Administration of charitable *awqaf* gave notables supervisory powers over substantial commercial and some agricultural properties in Hama and its countryside.[63] In addition, the personal wealth of notables and their families was also significant. In 1791, for instance, two children and a grandson of the prominent religious scholar al-Shaykh Ishaq al-Kaylani (d. 1185/1771–1772)[64] endowed as a family *waqf* a coffee

---

60 Muhammad al-Makki, *Tarikh Hims*, ed. and introduced by 'Umar Najib al-'Umar (Damascus, 1987), e.g. 20, 27–28, 52, 54, 60–61, 67.

61 E.g. Mustafa b. Ibrahim al-'Alwani (d. 1779–1780), who was born in Hama, studied in Damascus with the renowned Shaykh 'Abd al-Ghani al-Nabulsi, served as *naqib al-ashraf* of Hama, and after his dismissal from that post was in great demand as a teacher in Damascus. al-Sabuni, *Tarikh Hamah*, 167.

62 E.g. al-Shaykh 'Alwan mosque and Bimaristan al-Nuri. LCR Hama 46:127–128, doc. 265, 13 Jumada II 1206/ 7 Feb. 1792; al-Sabuni, *Tarikh Hamah*, 113.

63 al-Sabuni, *Tarikh Hamah*, 108–109.

64 Ibid. 166.

house that they owned in *mahallat* al-Madina.[65] Another coffee house in al-ʻAlaylat was owned (at least in part) by members of the ʻAlwani family.[66] Kaylanis owned shops in Suq al-Mansuriyya and al-Hadir,[67] plus luxurious houses in al-Hadir,[68] shops, gardens, the ʻAdiliyya coffee house, an artisanal workshop, water mills, a public bath, and residential compounds (*ahwash*).[69] Individuals of notable status often had diverse property interests; Salih b. Ahmad al-ʻAlwani left an estate that included a large house, a bakery, a share of the ʻAlaylat coffee house, and half an orchard, half a shop, and two groves (sing. *karm*) in al-Ribah village.[70] Ahmad b. Hijazi al-ʻAlwani left houses and shares of an oven, a shop and the coffee house in al-ʻAlaylat, and lands and orchards in al-Ribah and Zawr al-Khamsa.[71] Notables also possessed mills; in 1792, for instance, the mufti and the *naqib* of Hama (both Kaylanis) jointly purchased a mill near Homs from villagers, local elites, and the mufti of Homs, all of whom owned shares.[72] In addition to owning mills (or possessing them via long-term *hikr* contracts), notables administered *awqaf* such as that of ʻAbd al-Qadir al-Kaylani whose properties included mills.[73]

In some instances, such as in the alimentary economy (food production and processing), elites and notables formed partnerships. For example, the mufti Ibrahim al-Kaylani and the agha of Shaykhun,

---

65 LCR Hama 46:113, doc. 233, 1 Muharram 1206/ 31 Aug. 1791.

66 LCR Hama 46:205a, doc. 466 [pt. 2], *awakhir* Jumada II 1209/ 21 Jan. 1795.

67 E.g. ʻAbd al-Wahid b. ʻAbd al-Rahman al-Kaylani's purchase of four shops in al-Hadir for himself and his wife; and al-Shaykh ʻAbd al-Razzaq b. al-Shaykh Isma'il al-Kaylani's ownership of a carpenter's shop in Suq al-Mansuriyya in 1794. LCR Hama 46:174, docs. 367–368, 8 Rabiʻ II 1208/ 13 Nov. 1793; 46:186, doc. 412 [pt. 1], 4 Rajab 1208/ 5 Feb. 1794.

68 LCR Hama 46:253–254, doc. 542, 25 Dhu al-Qaʻda 1211/ 22 May 1797.

69 LCR Hama 46:251–253, doc. 541, 13 Dhu al-Qaʻda 1209/ 1 June 1795.

70 LCR Hama 46:380, doc. 681, 4 Shaʻban 1214/ 2 Jan. 1800.

71 LCR Hama 46:349–350, doc. 636, 21 Jumada II 1213/ 5 Dec. 1798. The word *zawr* referred to thickets of trees along the river valley. See Zakariyya, *ʻAsha'ir al-Sham*, 25.

72 LCR Hama 46:172, doc. 362, 10 Rabiʻ I 1267/ 26 Oct. 1792; 46:173, doc. 363, 10 Rabiʻ I 1207/ 26 Oct. 1792; 46:173–174, doc. 364, *awasit* Rabiʻ I 1207/ 31 Oct. 1792..

73 LCR Hama 46:134–135, doc. 278, 22 Safar 1207/ 9 Oct. 1792.

a caravansary and fortress on the road to Aleppo, had a farming and livestock partnership in the village of Kafr ‘Ayn for a period of time until 1793.[74] The existence of such partnerships, combined with examples of intermarriage and occupational diversity mentioned in the previous chapter, suggests that the interests of elites and religious notables ultimately were intertwined. The social functions of elites and notables were distinct, and they might engage in rivalries and power struggles among and between themselves, but in the final analysis their privileged status was jointly linked to Ottoman provincial and imperial political and legal structures.[75]

In the absence of local chronicles, it is difficult to know how these various social networks interacted in eighteenth-century Hama. Regrettably the picture depicted here is static and does not portray the society in motion. However, arguing from analogy with Hama’s better-known and better-documented cousins (Damascus and Aleppo), one can hypothesize that clientage ties and factional politics were characteristic of the social order, with different groups of elites and notables jockeying for political and material advantage under the eye of a less-than-omnipotent state. Ottoman authority in Damascus province reached its nadir in the years 1785–1812, when bitter factional struggles accompanied by rapidly rotating governorships and tribal challenges produced years of violence and political instability.[76] These struggles also engulfed Hama, where in 1788 townspeople rose up against an unpopular *mutasallim* causing the governor of Damascus to lead a punitive expedition and to disarm the population.[77] As a stronghold of the ‘Azm family, Hama could not but become a party to wider political conflicts in which the military (*mamluk*) household of Jazzar Pasha, based at Acre, attempted to extend its sway from the Syrian coast to the interior regions that were governed from Damascus.

---

74 LCR Hama 46:152, doc. 316, 5 Rabi‘ I 1208/ 11 Oct. 1793.

75 Cf. the copious evidence from eighteenth-century Damascus of economic and family links among merchants, military elites, and ‘ulama’. Establet and Pascual, *Familles et fortunes*, 136.

76 Douwes, *Ottomans in Syria*, chap. 4.

77 LCR Hama 46:57, doc. 138, 3 Jumada II 1202/ 11 March 1788; Yusuf, *Tarikh Hamah*, 33.

Social networks – consisting of de jure or de facto groupings of people according to religion, ethnicity, occupation, and residence – characterize the organization of Hama in the eighteenth and nineteenth centuries. However, the Hama evidence does not lend itself to an interpretation of social networks as discrete and mutually exclusive entities. Christians and Muslims lived in the same neighborhoods and worked in the same crafts. Networks based on religion, quarter, and craft were sources of identity and set parameters of behavior and of action. But which dimension of people's complex identities occupied the foreground varied according to context. With this in mind one should not automatically assume that political factionalism and ethnic-sectarian hostility were endemic or rampant in societies like Hama's.[78] Elites and notables had complex, parallel, and interlocking interests expressed via different social networks. In certain contexts a Kaylani shaykh, for instance, might act as a Sufi leader, or as a judicial official, or a *waqf* administrator, or a quarter notable, or a landowner. His elite counterpart (e.g. an 'Azm) might be a power broker, a landowner, the representative of a given urban quarter, a patron of the craft corporations, a partner of the Kaylani in a mill, or all of these things concurrently. Moreover, people of different social categories did not necessarily need intermediaries to deal with one another, as demonstrated by agreements that linked urban traders and merchants directly with rural bedouins.

---

78 An assumption found, for instance, in the work of University of Damascus historian Yusuf Jamil Nu'aysa, *Mujtama' Madinat Dimashq fi al-Fatra ma bayn 1186–1256 hijri 1772–1840 miladi*, 2 vols. (Damascus, 1986), 1:203, 264–265. See the brief critique and analysis in James A. Reilly, "Past and Present in Local Histories of the Ottoman Period from Syria and Lebanon," *Middle Eastern Studies* 35 (1999): 45–65.

Chapter Four: Population, Trade, and Manufactures

Throughout the Ottoman period Syria's economy was predominantly agricultural. Most people lived and worked in the countryside where they grew food crops or industrial crops destined for subsistence, for the tax collector, or for trade and sale in local and regional markets. Inter-regional trade, and a hierarchy of markets and market towns, linked rural regions to local centers such as Homs and Hama, and then on to the metropolises of Aleppo and Damascus and seaports of Saida and Tripoli. These regional trade routes supplied urban manufacturers of textiles, clothing, furniture and tools with the raw materials that they needed, and gave urban merchants and manufacturers access to the countryside for marketing goods that rural people did not manufacture themselves.

Although the Syrian lands met their own needs in the production of food, manufactures, and animal products – and exported these items to other part of the Ottoman Empire as taxes or merchandise – Syria was not aloof from wider currents affecting the Ottoman Empire. Aleppo's commercial profile, for instance, was closely connected to the development of Ottoman relations with Safavid Iran. During periods of peace or tranquility, Aleppo was a western entrepôt of the Iranian silk trade, for which purpose merchants from England, Venice and Genoa flocked to the city and established permanent centers. When Ottoman warfare with Iran disrupted the silk trade, Aleppine commerce risked setbacks and so compensatory trade was found by selling raw wool from the region of Aleppo to English merchants, especially. By the eighteenth century population and wealth were shifting from northern Syria – the region served by Aleppo – to coastal and central Syria, served and administered from Saida and Damascus, respectively. The reasons for this shift, as well as its scope and extent, are not entirely clear. They may be linked at least in part to trends in international trade. Following the collapse of Safavid authority in Iran (1722), political instability and border warfare with the Ottoman Empire ended the lucrative northern silk commerce. At about the same time, the southern regions of Syria profited from burgeoning French interest in the raw material of the coast – mainly cotton, but also silk – and the consolidation of political authority by the ʻAzm governors of Damascus through the 1750s. This was the context in which Hama and Homs found themselves drawn out of the economic orbit of a (relatively declining) Aleppo and transferred to the administration of Damascus.

The British blockade of France and Continental Europe during the Napoleonic Wars produced a sharp drop-off in Mediterranean trade. Following this hiatus, however, the Syrian lands were exposed to the full force of the Industrial Revolution and the changes in global trade and manufacturing that came in its wake from the 1820s onward. The integration of Syria into the European-centered capitalist world economy, the rapid repopulation of the coastal towns and regions, and the extension of industrial and commercial crops destined for export to Europe, affected the Syrian lands in their entirety. Although the most visible changes occurred in the coastal regions, the consequences of the Industrial Revolution were also felt in interior regions like Hama and Homs whose districts became agricultural hinterlands and suppliers to the bustling coastal towns. Forms of economic life in the Syrian interior were slow to change, but their economic relationships (e.g. between Hama and its hinterland, and between Hama and the coast) were significantly altered by these global economic transformations.[1]

During the Ottoman period Hama's economy reflected its location on the dividing line between the 'desert and the sown' in the central Syrian plain. Hama drew from its agricultural hinterland grain, silk, and foodstuffs, and traded these plus its manufactured goods with the pastoralists of the steppe. Although most of Hama's manufactures were destined for the town itself or its immediate hinterland, its silk textiles enjoyed a regional renown. Hama's location on major communications routes also contributed to its economic significance. Hama was linked to the sea via the port of Tripoli to the southwest, to Homs and Damascus in the south, and to Aleppo in the north. Caravans and pilgrims traveling between Aleppo and Damascus

---

1 Abdel-Nour, *Introduction*, 84, 317; Owen, *Middle East*, chaps 6 and 10, *passim*.

passed through Hama, creating opportunities for trade and commerce; at the same time, because the Aleppo–Damascus route was also a major military road, residents of Hama often found themselves pressed to pay special taxes and provide services for soldiers and officials.

Urban Growth and Changes in Population

The importance of Hama's link to the steppes is demonstrated by its pattern of growth during the Ottoman period. Though older accounts speak of economic regression,[2] more recent work suggests that Hama witnessed a secular expansion during the centuries of Ottoman rule.[3] Hama's growth was part of a general urban fluorescence in the Fertile Crescent that the Ottoman conquest facilitated by binding far-flung regions into a vast and relatively secure trading network.[4] At the Ottoman conquest Hama's center of gravity was located on the western bank of the Orontes River, in the shadow of its citadel. Hama's Great Mosque was also there, on the site of an earlier Byzantine church and a Roman temple. The major bridge for the Homs–Aleppo road crossed the Orontes at Shayzar, some 20 kilometers downstream from Hama. Shortly after Ottoman rule began, however, a new bridge rose at Hama that made it rather than Shayzar the principal middle-Orontes crossing point. Hama's new bridge, Jisr al-Hawa, was located north of the citadel hill and (like the older one at Shayzar) it was built sufficiently high to remain passable even during spring floods. The quarter of Bab al-Jisr ('Bridge Gate') developed around it, and Jisr al-Hawa facilitated Hama's expansion on to the right bank of the Orontes, namely al-Hadir and its extensions (al-Sharqiyya, Bayn al-Hayrayn, al-Barudiyya, al-Zanbaqi).

---

2 E.g. 'Ali al-Hasani, *Tarikh Suriya al-Iqtisadi* (Damascus, 1923–24), 139, 143.

3 Musa and Harba, *Muhafazat Hamah*, 233–236; Al-Dbiyat, "Homs et Hama," 210.

4 Raymond, *Grandes villes arabes*, 54–66.

The right-bank districts were characterized by their rural and bedouin connections, and they were settled in part by sedentarized nomads. Al-Hadir had its own market or *suq* that specialized in sheep products and craft production oriented to rural and pastoralist needs. By the eighteenth century Hama had 14 *khans* (caravansaries). Most of them – used for the storage and distribution of seeds, cotton, wool, and clarified butter – were located in al-Hadir, underscoring the key role of links to the steppe in the structure of Hama's urban economy. Within 100 years of the Ottoman conquest, the right-bank quarters had developed into a commercial center distinct from that of the older, left-bank quarters, collectively known as the Suq side. The important commercial character of al-Hadir (right bank) and al-'Alaylat (left bank) is evident in the neighborhood tax assessments of the 1730s reproduced in Appendix 1. By the end of the Ottoman period in the early twentieth century, multiple bridges formed links between the two banks of the river. These included (from north to south) al-Hawa, the fourteenth-century al-Afdal or Bayt al-Shaykh (a later appellation referring to the nearby mansion of 'Abd al-Qadir al-Kaylani), and al-Murakib (subsequently known as al-Saraya in reference to a later Ottoman administrative building). The advent of the railroad early in the twentieth century provided some impetus for westward expansion (on the Suq side) late in the Ottoman period.[5]

No precise population figures for Hama are available. For lack of better alternatives we must rely on assorted estimates, mostly from foreign observers, whose sources and methods of calculation were not consistent with each other. The French traveler Volney, who passed through Hama in the 1780s, offered an early estimate.[6] He put its population at 4,000, which is low in relation to most subsequent figures. Nineteenth- and early twentieth-century estimates are summarized in Table 1.

Wide variations among these figures signal that they must be used cautiously. The numbers cited do not even refer to the same

---

5 Musa and Harba, *Muhafazat Hamah*, 230–236, 418; Al-Dbiyat, "Homs et Hama," 210–211; Rafeq, "Mazahir iqtisadiyya," 52; Yusuf [Barghuth], "Tarikh Hamah," 12; Abdel Nour, *Introduction*, 317.

6 Volney, *Travels*, 2:297.

geographic area. Some population estimates referred only to the town itself, while others encompassed Hama's hinterland or even the entire administrative district of Hama (which included the town of Homs).

Table 1
Hama Population Estimates, 1812–1909

Year	**Estimate**	**Source**
1812	30,000	Burckhardt
1830	20,000	Robinson
1839	30–44,000	Bowring
1850s	30,000	Porter
1862	10–12,000	Guys
1880	27,656 (53,163)	Parliamentary Papers (1881)
1901	60,000	Parliamentary Papers (1902)
1907	80,000	Trade Reports (1908)
1906	40,000 (69,300)	al-Sabuni
1909	60,000	Trade Reports (1909)

SOURCES: John Lewis Burckhardt, *Travels in Syria and the Holy Land* (London, 1822), 146; George Robinson, *Voyage en Palestine et en Syrie*, 2 vols. (Paris, 1838), 2:327; John Bowring, *Report on the Commercial Statistics of Syria* (London, 1840), 7, 87; Henry Guys, *Esquisse de l'état politique et commercial de la Syrie* (Paris, 1862), 220; Great Britain, *Parliamentary Papers* (1902), 110:656; Great Britain, Foreign Office, *Trade Reports* 4080 (1908), 3; J. L. Porter, *The Giant Cities of Bashan, and Syria's Holy Places* (London, 1866), 305; Ahmad al-Sabuni, *Tarikh Hamah* (Hama, 1956), 101; Great Britain, Foreign Office, *Trade Reports* 4293 (1909), 2.

In Table 1, Robinson's figures refer only to Hama town. Bowring gives two separate figures without explanation, but they appear to refer to Hama town (30,000), on the one hand, and Hama plus its village hinterland (44,000 total) on the other. The low estimate offered by Guys (10–12,000) in all likelihood refers only to Hama town. The 1880 figures from British consular sources report a town population of 27,656, and a total *district* population (including Homs) of nearly twice that. The British sources of 1902, 1908, and 1909 do not specify whether their figures refer only to Hama proper, or (what is more likely) Hama plus its farming hinterland. The local historian al-Sabuni is the only one of these who gives an indication of his figures' reliability. He derived them from Ottoman census figures that indicated an urban population of 40,000 and a village hinterland population of 29,300. However, al-Sabuni cautioned that the village figures are significantly understated, explaining that villagers mistrustful of the government sought to conceal themselves from census takers. He adds that bedouins (*'urban*) living in the rural districts were not counted at all.[7]

Despite variations among these estimates, the overall population trend in the eighteenth and nineteenth centuries was upward. Hama experienced continued growth in the later Ottoman period, marked by the appearance of new quarters such as the Hamidiyya and the expansion of the town westward in the direction of the railroad line (opened 1902).[8] To be sure, population numbers could fluctuate, sometimes dramatically. For instance, an outbreak of plague followed by an infestation of locusts reportedly killed up to one-half of the inhabitants of Homs and Hama in 1826.[9] Al-Sabuni, for his part, notes that the population of Hama fell markedly in the first four decades or so of the nineteenth century due to its rulers' oppression and misgovernment:

> This situation continued until most of Hama's residents had fled to Damascus, and others to Aleppo, Homs and Tripoli. Hama's buildings and population dwindled and it came to resemble a village. Then Ibrahim Pasha the Egyptian arrived and misfortunes multiplied.[10]

But al-Sabuni then goes on to say that Hama's population resumed its growth after the end of Egyptian rule in 1840.[11]

Thus Hama experienced an overall growth in the aftermath of the sixteenth-century Ottoman conquest, despite evidence of contraction during the Ottoman troubles of the late sixteenth century and part of

---

7 al-Sabuni, *Tarikh Hamah*, 102.
8 Musa and Harba, *Muhafazat Hamah*, 236.
9 As'ad, *Tarikh Hims*, 2:373.
10 al-Sabuni, *Tarikh Hamah*, 85.
11 Ibid.

the seventeenth century.[12] This growth was especially pronounced on the right bank of the Orontes River where al-Hadir formed the nucleus of a second commercial center that benefited from close relations with peoples of the steppe, and that complemented the older manufacturing and market centers of the Suq on the left bank. The upward trend appears to have continued through the mid-eighteenth century, when Hama became a regional base for the al-ʻAzm family whose rule helped Damascus to wrest much regional trade away from Aleppo. However, the general crisis that shook the Syrian lands from the mid-eighteenth century onward also touched Hama. Insecurity on trade routes, pastoral nomadic incursions linked to the northward migration of the ʻAnaza bedouin from Arabia, and military expenses caused by wars with the Mamluk beys of Egypt and Bonaparte's invading army, inflicted considerable hardship on Hama's people. By the early decades of the nineteenth century the town's population had declined due to sickness, famine, fear and flight. Nevertheless the subsequent combination of greater security, improved communications, and increased demand for the products of Hama's agricultural hinterland all contributed to a period of growth and relative prosperity in the last two-thirds of the nineteenth century.

Manufacturing and Services

Al-Barghuth's pioneering but unpublished study of eighteenth-century Hama enumerates 43 craft corporations in the town, compared to 70 corporations two centuries before.[13] This diminution in the number of craft corporations over two centuries may signal a reduction in output. Conversely, it may simply point to a consolidation of disparate functions within craft corporations or the disappearance of certain craft

12 Abdel Nour, *Introduction*, 321.

13 Yusuf [Barghuth], "Tarikh Hamah," 53; idem, "Tawa'if al-hiraf wa-al-sinaʻat fi al-qarn al-sadis ʻashar," cited in Musa and Harba, *Muhafazat Hamah*, 373–374.

specializations. Al-Barghuth's eighteenth-century list mentions a variety of trades and services. Prominent among them were manufacturers of gunpowder (the *barudiyya*) whose industry had been established by the Ottomans in the sixteenth century and whose output was destined for military garrisons as far away as Tripoli.[14] Other manufacturing trades met the needs of local customers in town and the hinterland. These included blacksmiths, cobblers, coppersmiths, apothecaries, tanners, chandlers, farriers, turners, saddlers, mat-weavers, tent-weavers, rope-makers, carpenters, fodder-vendors, and makers of assorted agricultural implements. A second category of craft workers prepared or marketed foodstuffs, including bakers, butchers, oil-press operators, sweets-makers, and vendors of hummus and of grilled meat. Craft corporations linked to textile manufacture included those of spinners, weavers, wool-drapers, cotton-sellers, dyers, fullers, makers of woolen cloaks (sing. *'aba'a*), and cord-and-trim makers. Moneychangers, jewelers, and merchants also had discrete craft corporations.

Al-Barghuth's enumeration contains curious gaps, however. Where, for instance, are the barbers (sing. *hallaq*)? Their trade certainly was known in Hama.[15] Other 'missing' trades include millers (sing. *tahhan*) and operators of oil-presses, public baths and coffee-houses. It is possible that these missing trades simply were not organized into corporations; but a comparison of al-Barghuth's text with the primary sources that he used (the Islamic law-court registers of Hama) reveals the names of some corporations that he inexplicably left out of his enumeration. These include furriers, coffee-sellers, and manufacturers of clarified butter and of linen.[16] Therefore, Hama's craft corporations in the eighteenth century probably numbered at least fifty.

---

14 LCR Hama 46:263, doc. 552, 26 Rabi' I 1213/ 7 Sept. 1798; Musa and Harba, *Muhafazat Hamah*, 373–374.

15 E.g. the estate of the barber Muhammad b. Qaddur, d. 1793. LCR Hama 46:152, doc. 317, 27 Safar 1208/ 4 Oct. 1793.

16 LCR Hama 46:53, doc. 130, 5 Jumada I 1202/ 12 Feb. 1788; 46:177, doc. 373, Rajab 1208/ Feb.-March 1794; 46:243, doc. 569, 8 Rajab 1211/ 7 Jan. 1797.

Craft corporations in Ottoman Syria had long pedigrees, and they were descended from two pre-Ottoman phenomena. First were the fraternal societies known as (sing.) *futuwwa*, whose form and structure resembled those of Sufi mystical orders. The second was the regulation of markets and mercantile activities through officials and headmen answerable to the Mamluk sultans who had governed Syria and Egypt prior to the Ottomans' arrival.[17] Here as in other aspects of social and economic life, the new Ottoman rulers built upon and developed what they had inherited. With Ottoman rule, craft corporations acquired formal recognition and structure, and they played defined roles in urban economic life. Corporations were responsible for controlling entry into specialized occupations, training and certifying craftsmen, delivering taxes assessed on crafts, exercising quality control, and (in the case of alimentary and strategic goods) ensuring the availability of adequate supplies at administered prices. Each corporation was headed by a shaykh selected (in principle, at least) by the craftsmen but answerable to the Ottoman governor or his deputies.[18] Corporations encompassed the major part of the economically active male population of Syrian towns. Linked as they were historically and ritualistically with Sufism, they were also important social organizations that at one and the same time could mobilize and represent the male working population. Here too Hama presents patterns that are evocative or reminiscent of those in other Syrian centers.

The character of craft corporations as fiscal and regulatory units is evident in the corporation of gunpowder manufacturers. Gunpowder manufacturing was established in Hama by the Ottoman authorities,[19] and the corporation of gunpowder manufacturers was responsible for the annual provision of gunpowder supplies to various garrisons.[20] The corporations also served as instruments of government economic regulation, particularly regarding the crucial matter of food supplies

---

17 Gabriel Baer, *Egyptian Guilds in Modern Times*, (Jerusalem, 1964), 7–8; Lapidus, *Muslim Cities*, 97–99.

18 Abdul-Karim Rafeq, "Craft Organization, Work Ethics, and the Strains of Change in Ottoman Syria," *Journal of the American Oriental Society* 111 (1991): 496–497.

19 Musa and Harba, *Muhafazat Hamah*, 373–374.

20 E.g. LCR Hama 46:263, doc. 552, 26 Rabi' I 1213/ 7 Sept. 1798.

and prices. Taxes owed by butchers' shops, for instance, were linked to the 'generally known costs' of different categories of meat; the head of the butchers' corporation, the *qassab bashi*, was a significant figure in the economic administration of the town.[21] There is a parallel here between the Ottoman administration of Hama and that of Jerusalem,[22] underscoring the importance that the Ottoman administration placed on the supply and price of meat. Consistent with this concern for urban food supplies and prices, the corporation of bakers (*khabbazin*) also acted as a regulatory arm of the administration. The *khabbazin* were compelled to pledge in 1728 that they would use only good wheat to make their product and that they would be mindful of the needs of the poor. Failure to meet these standards would subject them to severe corporal punishment.[23] Since the bakers were compelled to make this pledge, it is likely that some of them had, in fact, sold an adulterated product thus failing to meet requisite norms of social responsibility for the destitute (*al-fuqara'*). By compelling bakers to promise good-quality bread, the local Ottoman administration publicly demonstrated its commitment to 'justice': viz., in return for its privileges, the ruling class was supposed to be mindful of the subsistence needs of the poor.

The local administration also regulated economic activities that were not essential for subsistence, but that answered to the needs of the treasury. A good example is provided by a petition drawn up in 1795 from the corporation of sweets-makers (*al-halwaniyya*). Representatives of the corporation complained to Hama's district governor that, for five years, his predecessors had obliged them to pay in advance for raisins produced by the inhabitants of five villages, in order that the latter could pay their taxes. These forced loans exceeded the value of the raisins that the sweets-makers eventually obtained. As a consequence, their petition continued, they faced ruin and many were abandoning the business altogether. The sweets-makers appealed

21 LCR Hama 46:237–238, docs. 519–520, Sha'ban 1210/ Feb.–March 1796; LCR Hama 42:325, doc. 658, 10 Shawwal 1144/ 6 April 1732; 46:243, doc. 569, 8 Rajab 1211/ 7 Jan. 1797.

22 Cohen, *Economic Life*, chap. 1, *passim*.

23 LCR Hama 42:310, doc. 626, 7 Rabi' I 1141/ 11 Oct. 1728.

to the district governor to end this advance-payment requirement. He did so, labeling the payments a 'harmful innovation' contrary to the interests of the treasury.[24] In this instance, the corporation of sweets-makers served both as an instrument of government administration (by requiring the *halwaniyya* to make high advance payments to villagers), and as a body that appealed on behalf of the sweets-makers to the administration. The sweets-makers' story underscores the twofold character of the corporations, which were expected to represent the authorities to their membership, and their membership to the authorities, a role that they continued to play into the nineteenth century.[25]

Other instances of the corporations acting as group representatives vis-à-vis the local administration include an example from 1732, when delegations from craft corporations or occupational groups as well as from urban quarters complained of financial hardship and petitioned the district governor for tax relief. The groups or corporations represented in these delegations included merchants, the *qassab bashi* (head of the butchers' corporation), fodder-sellers (*'allafin*), and the bakers, all of whom were held responsible for providing goods or specie to support the military forces.[26]

Even though gunpowder was the most important manufacture of eighteenth-century Hama from the Ottoman government's perspective, textiles were the most significant handicraft industry. Some of the different craft corporations linked to various aspects of textile production were noted above. The textile trade was well established at Hama, and in the eighteenth century more workshops were devoted to weaving than to any other single craft.[27] Weaving retained its importance in Hama into the next century.[28] The textile industry in its

---

24 LCR Hama 46:215, doc. 482, 20 Ramadan 1209/ 10 April 1795.

25 E.g. when the corporation of apothecaries representing 43 *'attarin* agreed to restrict the sale of rat poison in the interests of public safety. LCR Hama 53:108, 14 Safar 1267/ 19 Dec. 1850.

26 LCR Hama 42:323, doc. 652, 12 Ramadan 1144/ 9 March 1732.

27 Rafeq, "Mazahir," 36; Yusuf [Barghuth], "Tarikh Hamah," 53–54; Anon., *Journey*, 31.

28 John Bowring, *Report on the Commercial Statistics of Syria* (London, 1840), 21; Guys, *Esquisse*, 220–221; Vital Cuinet, *Syrie Liban et Palestine:*

various forms created both backward and forward economic linkages, tying Hama to its rural hinterland and to regional markets.

In the eighteenth century cotton and silk were significant industrial crops in the Hama area. The importance of cotton cultivation – and probably also its extent – had grown since the Ottoman conquest two centuries before.[29] Cotton was produced to the northwest and southwest of Hama where Orontes irrigation was available, including Kafr Buhum, Kazu, and al-Rabi'a.[30] As for silk, mountain villagers raised silkworms in the hinterland of Hama – Jabal al-Kalbiyya, Shayzar, and al-Hisn – and southward into the hinterland of Tripoli.[31] Some of Hama's raw silk was exported to Europe via Tripoli, a trade that was locally significant but small compared to the much larger volume of Ottoman-European silk trade through the towns of Aleppo and Izmir.[32] Silk constituted a major source of tax revenue from the hill districts,[33] and the security of commerce in silk between Hama and Tripoli, on the one hand, and Hama and Aleppo on the other merited the personal attention of Hama's district governor.[34] Tripoli's hinterland continued to provide silk for Hama's looms in the nineteenth century.[35] The raising of silkworms was a cottage industry, and at least until the mid-nineteenth century ownership of mulberry plantations (leaves from which fed the silkworms) appears principally to have been in the hands of rural people.[36] While townspeople too owned mulberry plantations, cultivation and care of the trees required intensive labor. This requirement led urban owners to grant property

---

géographie administrative, statistique, descriptive et raisonnée (Paris, 1896), 366; Great Britain, Foreign Office, *Trade Reports* 4293 (1909), 5.

29 Cf. Rafeq, "Mazahir," 35; Yusuf [Barghuth], "Tarikh Hamah," 48–49; Volney, *Travels*, 2:297.

30 Yusuf [Barghuth], "Tarikh Hamah," 48–49.

31 Ibid. 49; al-Hasani, *Tarikh Suriya*, 139.

32 al-Hasani, *Tarikh Suriya*, 140; Masters, *Origins*, 28.

33 E.g. the district of al-Hisn in LCR 42:414, doc. 819, *awasit* Dhu al-Hijja 1146/ 19 May 1734.

34 E.g. LCR Hama 46:117, doc. 241, 12 Safar 1206/ 11 Oct. 1791; 46:118, doc. 244, 15 Safar 1206/ 14 Oct. 1791.

35 Guys, *Esquisse*, 93.

36 E.g. LCR Hama 53:62, 24 Shawwal 1266/ 2 Sept. 1850; 53:108, 15 Safar 1267/ 20 Dec. 1850.

rights to farmers in return for the latter's improvement of the property.[37] Here once again Hama offers an example of a wider Syrian pattern in which tenants established rights and even ownership of lands and crops requiring intensive work.[38]

Merchants organized and coordinated spinning and weaving activities, serving as links between suppliers of raw material and providers of labor.[39] Spinning and weaving were characterized by a gendered division of work: women spun and men wove, and spinners and weavers alike owned their own tools.[40] Hama's weavers used wool, cotton, silk, and threads of silver and gold to manufacture textiles for local and regional markets.[41] Among the most important cotton products were bath towels of various sizes and designs, and 'strongly woven' indigo-dyed linens.[42] Also made in Hama were shawls (sing. *zunnar*) used as waistbands woven in a variety of materials, including all-cotton, silk and cotton mixtures, pure silk and silk embroidered with silver and gold threads.[43] According to a British report prepared in 1888, Hama ranked with Damascus as a major Syrian center of silk and cotton weaving.[44] Cuinet's report of a few years later ranked Hama third (after Damascus and Homs) in terms of active looms and weavers in the province of Damascus. Cuinet's numbers are summarized below:

---

37 LCR Hama 53:13, Muharram 1266/ Nov.–Dec. 1849.

38 James A. Reilly, "Status Groups and Propertyholding in the Damascus Hinterland," *International Journal of Middle East Studies* 21 (1989): 517–539.

39 E.g. two prosperous merchants who died a few years apart. One specialized in raw silk and the other in both finished and unfinished cloth. LCR Hama 46:129, doc. 268, 15 Rajab 1206/ 9 March 1792; 46:379–380, doc. 676, 4 Sha'ban 1214/ 2 Jan. 1800.

40 E.g. LCR 42:338, doc. 691, *awakhir* Dhu al-Qa'da 1144/ 25 May 1732; 46:159, doc. 334 [part 1], *salkh* Rabi' I 1208/ 5 Nov. 1793; 46:264, doc. 555, 29 Rabi' II 1213/ 10 Oct. 1798; 53:23, 19 Rabi' I 1266/ 2 Feb. 1850; 53:82, 22 Dhu al-Qa'da 1266/ 29 Sept. 1850; 53:259, 23 Shawwal 1268/ 10 Aug. 1852.

41 Bowring, *Report*, 21, 136.

42 Guys, *Esquisse*, 220–221.

43 Cuinet, *Syrie*, 367; al-Hasani, *Tarikh Suriya*, 216.

44 Great Britain, *Parliamentary Papers* (1889), 81:104.

Table 2
Looms and Weavers in Damascus Province, 1896

Town	Looms	Weavers
Damascus	3,000	21,000
Homs	4,000	28,000
Hama	700	4,900

SOURCE: Vital Cuinet, *Syrie Liban et Palestine: géographie administrative, statistique, descriptive et raisonnée* (Paris, 1896), 366.

One decade later, yet another British report asserted that the combined total of weavers in Homs and Hama exceeded the number of those ('more than 10,000') working in Damascus, and that the total textile output of Homs and Hama together was more than twice that of Damascus.[45] Although the precise figures offered by these French and British sources may not be reliable, nevertheless they give some idea of the scale of Hama's textile industry. Weaving employed comparable numbers of people in Damascus and Hama as a proportion of each town's total population (Hama: 4,900 textile workers among a population of ca. 60,000; Damascus: 21,000 textile workers among a population of 250,000). In both Damascus and Hama, weaving and its ancillary trades and crafts formed the single most important occupational sector of the urban economy.

Besides textiles woven from cotton and silk, Hama also was known for its woolen products. Like cotton and silk weaving, the manufacture of woolens created backward and forward linkages with regional economies. Hamawis obtained their wool from bedouins, Kurds and Turcomans who came to Hama's markets.[46] In the mid-nineteenth century approximately one-fifth of the wool brought to Hama was used in local manufacturing, including rugs, woolen cloaks (*'aba'as*), felt hats and saddle blankets, and inexpensive bedding.[47]

45 Great Britain, *Trade Reports* 4293 (1909), 5.
46 Bowring, *Report*, 16.
47 Guys, *Esquisse*, 221.

These products were sold in town, in the villages, and especially to the pastoralists who frequented Hama's markets. Burckhardt signaled the importance of the pastoralists when he visited Hama in 1812 and wrote: 'The principal trade of Hamah is with the Arabs [bedouins], who buy here their tent furniture and clothes.'[48] Raw wool not used locally was exported to Europe via Tripoli.[49]

Although the formal sector of the craft economy (organized into corporations) was exclusively male,[50] women also contributed to production via the household economy. Evidence of women's work includes their ownership of spinning wheels and (more rarely) weaving looms.[51] Hence the weaving industry for which Hama was known[52] depended on the (unorganized) labor of women, who by spinning and weaving contributed to household subsistence. Though they were not members of craft corporations, women could be known for their mastery of a trade; for instance 'Ruqayya the seamstress' who is mentioned in a document from 1797.[53] Ownership of shops, and income therefrom, were predominantly in the hands of men. Women rarely owned shops, but even when they did they did not run the shops nor did they practice the trades associated with them.

Two nineteenth-century documents signal shops owned by women. One, Fatima bint 'Ali Kallush, owned a shop connected to the farrier's trade (*baytara*), and she authorized her husband to sell the shop to a practicing farrier. There is no indication that Fatima personally practiced the trade or intervened in the business. It is more likely that she had inherited the shop from a relative and then asked her

---

48 Burckhardt, *Travels*, 147.

49 France, *Bulletin consulaire français* (1879), 646.

50 All members of craft corporations whose names have been recorded are men. E.g. LCR Hama 42:310, doc. 626, 7 Rabi' I 1141/ 11 Oct. 1728; 42:325, doc. 658, 10 Shawwal 1144/ 6 April 1732; 46:159, doc. 335, 6 Rabi' II 1208/ 11 Nov. 1794; 53:108, 14 Safar 1267/ 19 Dec. 1850.

51 LCR Hama 42:338, doc. 691, *awakhir* Dhu al-Qa'da 1144/ 25 May 1732; 46:159, doc. 334 [pt. 1], *salkh* Rabi' I 1208/ 5 Nov. 1793; 46:264, doc. 555, 29 Rabi' II 1213/ 10 Oct. 1798; 53:82, 22 Dhu al-Qa'da 1266/ 29 Sept. 1850.

52 al-Hasani, *Tarikh Suriya*, 214; Guys, *Esquisse*, 220–221.

53 LCR Hama 46:244, doc. 530, 6 Rajab 1211/ 5 Jan. 1797.

husband to sell it for its cash value.[54] The second instance is recorded in two separate documents generated nearly three years apart. Ruqayya bint al-Sayyid ‘Abdallah al-Tarabulsi had inherited an indigo dye-shop from her father, and she was fending off attempts by a man who claimed to be the rightful owner to take possession of it. Ruqayya attended the court in person to obtain the requisite legal injunctions.[55] Ruqayya reiterated her ownership of the dye shop at least twice in a three-year period, a fact which suggests that she took an interest in the profession if only as a source of rental income.

Hama in the first half of the nineteenth century differed from Aleppo and Damascus, whose court records often noted women's ownership of shops and of licenses (sing. *gedik*) to practice trades.[56] The Hama registers surveyed do not mention licenses, which were a form of heritable and alienable property in Aleppo and Damascus. *Gedik* in Hama may have been embedded in shop ownership, and therefore (in local usage) did not need specific mention in property deeds. (In cases of endowment-owned shops, of which there were many, *gedik* belonged to the endowment for the use of whoever legally rented the endowment's property.) The effect of these practices or assumptions was to restrict women's access to ownership of commercial properties in Hama more than in Damascus or Aleppo.

The processes of wool, cotton and silk manufacturing and marketing underscore the integral economic links between Hama and its hinterland, with the latter Hama's source of raw materials and a market for its products. Other Hama manufactures that found their way into regional villages included metalwork and jewelry.[57] So if Hama's

---

54 LCR Hama 53:6, 18 Dhu al-Qa‘da 1265/ 5 Oct. 1849.

55 LCR 53:14, 14 Muharram 1266/ 30 Nov. 1849; 53:271, 17 Shawwal 1268/ 4 Aug. 1852.

56 Margaret L. Meriwether, "Women and Economic Change in Nineteenth-Century Syria: The Case of Aleppo," in *Arab Women: Old Boundaries, New Frontiers*, ed. Judith E. Tucker (Bloomington, 1993), 73; James A. Reilly, "Women in the Economic Life of Late-Ottoman Damascus," *Arabica* 42 (1995): 85–86.

57 E.g. the clothing, sword, jewelry, and iron and copperware that were among the inheritance of a wealthy villager of al-Jurniyya, who died in 1850. LCR Hama 53:86, 25 Dhu al-Hijja 1266/ 22 Oct. 1850.

agricultural surpluses were the great source of wealth for Hama's elite, nevertheless the health of the local economy depended too on its residents' employment in manufacturing and services. A geographer who has studied the Homs and Hama region, Mohamed Al-Dbiyat, argues that in the nineteenth century people of Hama were able to live more or less autonomously of the distant countryside, particularly in view of the fact that the town's immediate environs were fertile and supported truck farming. He further suggests that Hama's principal commercial activities were linked to long-distance trade.[58] I cannot fully agree with Al-Dbiyat on this score, because Hama was very much linked to its countryside not only for foodstuffs (that could, admittedly, be brought from the immediate fertile environs,)[59] but especially for the raw materials used in cotton, silk, and wool manufacturing.

Trade

Nevertheless, Al-Dbiyat certainly is on the mark when he contends that long-distance trade was important to Hama. The town's principal trading axes were with Aleppo, on the one hand, and Tripoli, on the other. From Aleppo, Hama's goods were carried onward to Anatolia and Iraq. From Tripoli they were shipped across the Mediterranean to Italy and France. In addition, because of its location on the pilgrimage route from Aleppo to Mecca via Damascus, Hama was annually visited by pilgrims and travelers going to and from the Hijaz. These pilgrimage caravans were an important impetus to Hama's trade through most of the Ottoman period,[60] and 'the pilgrimage road' was

58 Mohamed Al-Dbiyat, "Homs et Hama en Syrie centrale: bipole ou doublet urbaine?" (Ph.D. dissertation, Université de Tours, 1992), 34.

59 E.g. a vegetable garden in suburban Hama, the crops of which are listed in LCR Hama 46:117, doc. 242, 13 Safar 1206/ 12 Oct. 1792.

60 Rafeq, "Mazahir iqtisadiyya," *passim*; idem, "Qafilat al-hajj al-shami wa-ahammiyyatuha fi al-'ahd al-'uthmani," *Dirasat Tarikihiyya* no. 6 (1981), passim; Yusuf [Barghuth], "Tarikh Hamah," 62–63.

a geographic reference point in Hama.[61] Finally, Hama served also as a transit point for overland caravans linking Aleppo and Anatolia with Egypt. Egyptians passed through Hama and some took up residence there from at least the late eighteenth century onward.[62] In the nineteenth century improvements in communications, including the introduction of steamship travel, helped to intensify the already long-standing commercial relations between Syria and Egypt.

Trade generated by the pilgrimage caravans contributed to the growth of Hama in the Ottoman period. Under a single political authority following the consolidation of Ottoman rule, peoples of Anatolia and the Hijaz communicated with each other via Syria, including Hama. Rafeq has demonstrated the significance of the pilgrimage to the cash economy of Hama in the sixteenth century, when pilgrims traded and borrowed money in Hama to finance their journeys.[63] Venetian merchants also came in the sixteenth century to exchange broadcloth for cotton from Hama's irrigated hinterland.[64] The Venetians probably came from Aleppo, three days' caravan ride away,[65] where they and other foreign merchants had a permanent presence. During the eighteenth century, Hama textiles were carried to regional and international markets. Its sashes were traded with Baghdad and Iran through Aleppo,[66] and its linens were sent to Mediterranean and European markets via Tripoli.[67] An English visitor in 1725 commented favorably on Hama's commercial character.[68] This visitor (perhaps a merchant himself) was by no means unique; European traders were active in Hama during the eighteenth century, and local documents referred to them generically as *ta'ifat* al-Afranj,

---

61 LCR Hama 42:409, doc. 811, *muntasif* Rajab 1146/ 1 Jan. 1734.

62 E.g. LCR Hama 46:149, doc. 311, 24 Safar 1208/ 1 Oct. 1793; 46:186, doc. 412 [pt. 2], 5 Rajab 1208/ 6 Feb. 1794; 53:38, 9 Rajab 1266/ 21 May 1850; 53:55, *khitam* Ramadan 1266/ 9 Aug. 1850; 53:61, 14 Dhu al-Qa'da 1266/ 21 Sept. 1850.

63 Rafeq, "Mazahir iqtisadiyya," 27–29, 38.

64 Ibid. 18.

65 *Journey*, 22–28.

66 al-Hasani, *Tarikh Suriya*, 216.

67 *Journey*, 31.

68 Ibid.

‘the corporation of Franks.’ These ‘Franks’ were principally interested in buying Hama textiles and spun cotton. Comprised of various nationalities, the Franks included Venetians and Neapolitans, and they worked through agents or middlemen.[69]

Partnerships between foreign and local traders, and their links to Aleppo, are evident in a court document from 1791 reporting on the theft and recovery of silk from an Aleppo-bound caravan. On 14 October 1791, thirteen merchants of Aleppo appeared before Hama’s Islamic law court. They numbered three Muslims and ten Christians. Two of the Christians represented foreign trading communities (Swedes and Neapolitans). They reported that ‘villainous bedouins’ (*ashqiya’ al-‘urban*) had robbed their Aleppo-bound caravan, which included raw silk and a load of sashes that belonged to one of the merchants, Jurmanus al-Mutran. Hama’s *mutasallim*, Wafa Agha, had recovered the silk for them, so the merchants thanked him for his meritorious deed.[70]

The importance that Ottomans placed on trade and commerce is reflected in the string of caravansaries or *khans* which were maintained along trade routes through pious endowments established by high officials. The aforementioned English traveler of 1725 praised the caravansaries in which he stopped during his journey from Aleppo to Damascus via Hama. His description of the one at Ma‘arra (extant as a museum today) is worth recounting at length:

> The upper part of the building contains handsome rooms, which are reserved for the principal merchants and officers of the Karawân: underneath which is a portico or colonnade with Mastabez, or floors raised two or three feet from the ground, and there the common travelers are lodged [...] The Khân is capable of lodging 800 passangers [sic] and their horses with a great deal of ease. It is of that sort of inns which are endowed by their Founders, where a traveller may have bread, pilaw and mutton *gratis*; adjoining to the Khân is a Bagnio, and a street containing a coffee-house and five or six shops on each side. At the farther end of this street is an aquaduct [sic], which conveys the water into the Bagnio.[71]

---

69 Yusuf [Barghuth], “Tarikh Hamah,” 66–67.
70 LCR Hama 46:118, doc. 244, 15 Safar 1206/ 14 Oct. 1791.
71 *Journey*, 25.

As already noted, provincial governors had a personal pecuniary interest in trade, as evidenced by one Damascus governor's ownership of a covered marketplace in Hama, and a subsequent Damascus governor's proprietary interest in a caravansary at Qunaytira on the route from Damascus to Palestine and Egypt.[72]

Security of trade was a major concern for Ottoman officialdom. The safety of merchants and pilgrims was a measure of an administrator's success or failure. The governor of Damascus was responsible for the Mecca pilgrimage caravan, and the certificates of appointment from Damascus for Hama's *mutasallims* specified, *inter alia*, that they were to ensure the safety of pilgrims and travelers.[73] But as the silk theft mentioned above testifies, ensuring the safety of trade routes was not easy. Security in the Syrian steppes deteriorated during the eighteenth century due to factors and pressures that were outside the control of Ottoman rulers, including the northward migration of 'Anaza bedouin. Caravansaries suffered the vicissitudes of the times; when travelling in the rebel-dominated countryside between Aleppo and Hama in 1812, Burckhardt complained that Khan Tuman on the Kuwayk river was 'in a bad state; Pashas no longer think of repairing public edifices.'[74]

Hama provided significant support to the annual pilgrimage caravan. Local officials contracted Sakhana living in their eponymous quarter of Hama to carry supplies (*mu'nat al-jarda*) to returning pilgrims.[75] The governor of Damascus also rented camels in the Hama district to help convey pilgrims and their goods to and from the Hijaz. One example of such a transaction is preserved in a court document from 1797, in which al-Shaykh Ibrahim b. al-Shaykh Du'as let out 90 Arabian camels for this purpose to 'Abdallah Pasha al-'Azm, Amir al-Hajj and governor of Damascus. Most of the leased camels were ear-

72 LCR Hama 46:96–97, doc. 196, 3 Rabi' I 1204/ 21 Nov. 1789; LCR Damascus 312:33–34, doc. 102, 3 Rabi' I 1244/ 13 Sept. 1828.

73 E.g. Wafa Agha's letter of appointment in LCR Hama 46:79–80, doc. 173, 5 Jumada II 1203/ 3 March 1789.

74 Burckhardt, *Travels*, 121.

75 Yusuf [Barghuth], "Tarikh Hamah," 62.

marked to reach Mecca, with others contracted to go only as far as Medina and the fortress of Hadiyya before Medina.[76]

Individual legacies and inheritances demonstrate Hama's connections to its adjoining regions in the eighteenth and nineteenth centuries. For example, in 1794 a trader from the coastal town of Jabla died at Hama.[77] The contents of his legacy (cash, pack animals, weights and measures) suggest that he had come to Hama to purchase goods to sell at home or on his way back there. His house in Jabla, valued at 67 piasters, was far from opulent (the average price for a dwelling in Hama during this period was around 310 piasters), a fact which suggests that the deceased trader (al-Hajj 'Abidin al-Jablawi) may have been an itinerant peddler, serving small towns and villages en route from Hama to Jabla. On a grander scale was the legacy of the merchant and property-owner al-Sayyid Salih b. al-Sayyid Ahmad Efendi al-'Alwani, registered in the Hama court early in 1800.[78] Al-Sayyid Salih belonged to a mercantile branch of the notable al-'Alwani family. He had died at al-Nabk while en route to or from Damascus. The items in his legacy indicate that he was a cloth merchant. These items included bleached and raw silk that had been put out to female silk-reelers (*kabbabat*), raw cotton and two looms in the hands of his son 'Umar, and a considerable sum of gold in safekeeping with an associate in Damascus, one Ahmad Shakir. In addition to this al-Sayyid Salih had some commercial and agricultural properties and a residence in al-'Alaylat, the quarter of Hama with which the 'Alwani family were identified. Al-Sayyid Salih's legacy is indicative of the degree to which mercantile life in the city depended on its connections to other regions of Syria, including Aleppo (cotton), Hama's hinterland (silk), and Damascus (markets).[79] It is significant as well that a cloth merchant with diverse properties was affiliated to one of the notable families of Hama. This affiliation assured his access

76 LCR Hama 46:247, doc. 535, 2 Ramadan 1211/ 1 March 1797.

77 LCR Hama 46:193, doc. 436, 11 Sha'ban 1208/ 14 March 1794.

78 LCR Hama 46:379–380, doc. 676, 4 Sha'ban 1214/ 2 Jan. 1800.

79 Damascus as a destination for Hama leathers is indicated in a later document, LCR Hama 53:89, *khitam* Dhu al-Hijja 1266/ 5 Nov. 1850.

to a sympathetic legal system, enhanced his social prestige, and gave him an avenue (through relatives) to political authority.

Political connections were helpful to merchants, especially when local officials were tempted to treat them merely as a source of ready cash. Friction of this sort is evident in a reprimand that the governor of Damascus sent to his subordinates in Hama in January 1799. The governor noted that 'merchants of Hama' (*tujjar* Hamah) had complained that they faced ruin as a consequence of forced loans imposed on them by previous *mutasallims*. He ordered Hama's officials to cease this practice.[80] The background to this particular circular is unknown. Damascus governors of the period were not averse to tyrannical behavior themselves, and official extortion of money and foodstuffs from merchants would not have disturbed a governor such as the notorious al-Jazzar. Indeed, the author of this circular could well have been al-Jazzar himself. He may have been using a complaint from 'merchants of Hama' to remind local officials that he was the principal robber baron, and that they should watch their step. By intervening in this manner the governor of Damascus acted less to protect the subject population than to put his subordinates on guard. Regardless of the particular circumstances that gave rise to the governor's circular, it demonstrates that merchants, although vulnerable to exactions of rapacious officials, also depended on the Ottoman system for their livelihood and manipulated it to the best of their abilities. Affiliation with or relationships to local notable families were one means for a merchant to look out for his trading interests.

The variety of peoples from the Ottoman and Muslim lands who passed through Hama as pilgrims and traders is evident in the law-court records. Individual travelers from Daghistan, India, Anatolia, and Egypt all left traces in the law court registers of the mid-nineteenth century. The Daghistani died in Hama whilst en route from the Hijaz. He carried with him large numbers of prayer beads, perfumes and kohl from the holy land, perhaps to sell on his way back to the Caucasus region.[81] Two Egyptian peddlers quarreled over the

---

80 LCR Hama 46:259, doc. 546, 13 Sha'ban 1213/ 20 Jan. 1799.

81 LCR Hama 53:29, 16 Jumada II 1266/ 29 April 1850.

ownership their mule and their wares.[82] A traveler from the Anatolian district of Konya died in Hama, probably on his way to the Hijaz. He had on him a large quantity of specie, which was kept in trust by the law court until an heir could arrive to claim it.[83] The presence of such visitors in Hama points to its character as a transit point for travelers and trade. Others came from Anatolia and took up residence; such, for example, is the case of Ibish Agha b. ʻAli from Diyarbakir whose trading interests and activities extended to Aleppo and Alexandretta in the north to Damascus in the south.[84] Kurds from Anatolia, of whom Ibish Agha was one, had a long history of involvement in the important and lucrative trade in sheep and other livestock both in Hama and elsewhere in Syria.[85]

Thus Hama was at the hub of its own regional trading network, as well as a transit point in wider regional (and even international) networks. Hama was a manufacturing and marketing center for the bedouins of the steppe and for villagers who lived within its economic and political radius. Hama's long-distance trade depended on its situation as a transit point between larger administrative and economic centers (Damascus, Aleppo, and the port of Tripoli). In the course of time Hama's links to its rural hinterland and the subordination of villagers to urban elites would come to overshadow these other relationships and networks. The development of Hama into a center of large landed estates – a 'bastion of feudalism' – is the subject of the next two chapters.

82 LCR Hama 53:38, 9 Rajab 1266/ 21 May 1850.

83 LCR Hama 53:124, 1 Rabiʻ II 1267/ 3 Feb. 1851.

84 LCR Hama 53:127, 13 Rabiʻ II 1267/ 15 Feb. 1851.

85 Asʻad, *Tarikh Hims*, 2:332, 343, Bowring, *Report*, 16.

Chapter Five: Land, Rural Resources, and Debt

The land and its bounty were the principal sources of wealth in Ottoman Syria. The question of land once received much attention in the scholarly literature. Syrian land tenure patterns are an index of social stratification and class formation and they also are a sensitive barometer of the changing role of the Ottoman state at the local and provincial levels. However, land issues have received less attention in recent years as historians have moved on to new questions and problems posed by cultural studies, intellectual history and nationalism. Historiographic trends reflect their times: the flood of urbanization in the Middle East and in other developing societies during the later twentieth century has turned the spotlight away from the land, in contrast to histories written during the era of land reforms and 'peasant wars' in the 1950s–70s. Yet even though the subject has fallen out of favor, the development and legacy of Syria's land regime is critical for understanding the country's modern history. Few localities better illustrate this contention than Hama.

During the Ottoman period Hama was the administrative center of a fertile region – 'the granary of northern Syria' – whose agricultural hinterland in the eighteenth century included approximately 120 villages to the north, south, and west, the latter extending into the hills and valleys of the 'Alawi mountains.[1] Hama's principal agricultural products were grain from rain-fed steppes, cotton from irrigated areas in or near the Orontes valley, and silk from the

1 John Lewis Burckhardt, *Travels in Syria and the Holy Land* (London, 1822), 147. The 'granary' characterization is his. The Syrian historian Barghuth cites 51 as the number of villages around Hama in the mid-eighteenth century. This number may reflect the villages in Hama's direct hinterland, as distinct from the total that were administratively subordinate to the town. Yusuf [Barghuth], "Tarikh Hamah," 48–49. A French consular report from Damascus in 1842 gives the number of villages in Hama's district as 400, more than five times the comparable figure for Homs. This disproportionately high ratio is difficult to explain. AE, CC Damas 1.

mountains and foothills. Wool was a major product of the pastoral-nomadic economy.[2]

At the beginning of the twentieth century urban absentee land-holding was a marked feature of Hama. Mandate-era and subsequent writers alike have noted the sharp dichotomy that existed between Hama's large landowners on the one hand and its landless peasants, sharecroppers and villagers on the other.[3] This legacy affected the politics of Syria in the independence period, including the emergence of a peasant-based political movement in the Hama district in the 1950s which contributed to the formation of the later Ba'thist regime.[4] British Orientalist Gertrude Bell, who visited Hama in 1905, guessed that the power and influence of the landed families predated the nine-teenth-century consolidation of Ottoman rule in the countryside (which occurred under the aegis of the Tanzimat program of admin-istrative reforms).[5] However, studies of Hama and its region emphasize the relatively recent settlement of thinly populated steppes to the north and east of Hama in the second half of the nineteenth century by tribal cultivators, mountain peasants and Circassian refugees, part of a process whereby tribal shaykhs and urban absentees became major landholders with Ottoman government backing.[6] Contrasting accounts of the Hama steppe at different points in the nineteenth and early twentieth centuries underscore the drama and significance of this development. In remarks reminiscent of those made by eighteenth-century travelers such as Volney,[7] the British missionary Lyde portrayed the insecurity of life on the steppes, and

---

2 Volney, *Travels*, 2:297; Bowring, *Report*, 16; Guys, *Esquisse*, 220; AE, CC Damas 4, Hecquard, 16 Oct. 1862.

3 E.g. Muhammad Kurd 'Ali, *Khitat al-Sham*, 6 vols. (Damascus, 1925–28; reprint ed.: Damascus, 1983), 4:195; Jacques Weulersse, *Paysans de Syrie et du Proche-Orient* (Paris, 1946), 254–255; Al-Dbiyat, "Homs et Hama," 134–136; Musa and Harba, *Muhafazat Hamah*, 89.

4 Tabitha Petran, *Syria* (London, 1972), 87–89.

5 Bell, *Syria*, 224.

6 Al-Dbiyat, "Homs et Hama," 30, 33, 137; Norman N. Lewis, *Nomads and Settlers in Syria and Jordan, 1800–1980* (Cambridge UK, 1987), 69–70.

7 'The soil, as throughout this whole district, is well adapted to wheat and cotton; but agriculture, exposed to the rapine of the *Motsallam* and the Arabs, is in a very languishing condition.' Volney, *Travels*, 2:297.

painted a bleak prospect as he approached Hama from the north in 1853: ‘a wide plain, with neither tree nor shrub, but here and there some black Arab tents, or a village of mud-houses, like anthills.’ This view he contrasted with that of Hama itself: ‘the beautiful gardens laying on each side of the river, and abounding in fruit trees of every species.’[8] Within twenty years of the publication of these remarks, however, local authorities were auctioning land title-deeds to urban speculators.[9] By the end of the nineteenth century these authorities had unquestionably established government authority in the steppe. Writing in 1897, a French consular agent with close ties to the Homs and Hama districts noted that the Ottoman government exercised unprecedented control over the countryside in these districts, one consequence being increased agricultural productivity.[10] Grain cultivation had taken over these lands by the time of Gertrude Bell’s visit, when she saw ‘the monotonous plains of cornfields’ as she approached Hama and the Orontes valley.[11]

Despite the significance of these nineteenth-century transformations, the origins of large landholding in Hama did indeed predate settlement of the steppe. Urban elites and notables had already established their supremacy in portions of Hama’s hinterland during the eighteenth century. Their principal vehicle was the tax farm (*iltizam*), including lifetime tax farms known as (sing.) *malikane*. Tax farms did not, in and of themselves, confer ownership of rural areas to elites and notables. However, they did create a legally recognized group of landholders, of people and families who had access to rural

---

8 Samuel Lyde, *The Ansyreeh and Ismaeleeh: A Visit to the Secret Sects of Northern Syria* (London, 1853), 44–48, 55–56. See also Lewis, *Nomads*, 17. A century later the appearance of Hama still made a powerful impression: ‘C’est à Hama, la cité des norias, que ce type de paysage syrien atteint sa perfection; toute la basse ville y apparaît noyée dans la verdure, coupoles blanches entre les peupliers, tandis que la plainte grinçante des grandes roues ruisselantes y forme la basse continue du concert des bruits citadins.’ Weulersse, *L’Oronte*, 57.

9 AE, CC Damas 5, Robin, 8 Aug. 1872, 11 Jan. 1873.

10 AE, Nouvelle série (NS), Correspondance politique et commerciale, Turquie 105, P. Bambino (Beyrouth), 20 Nov. 1897.

11 Bell, *Syria*, 224.

surplus with approval and recognition of the state. Such approval could, in principle, be revoked if the tax farmers failed to make requisite payments, or if they fell out of political favor.

The Ottoman authorities had a keen interest in Hama's grain; eighteenth-century circulars from the governor of Damascus to his subordinates in Hama reminded them of standing orders to collect wheat and barley in government storehouses, and sternly warned them against pilfering and illegal sales (a telltale sign that this was a source of elites' personal enrichment).[12] In the absence of evidence to the contrary, the prevailing Ottoman pattern of village cultivation carried out by an independent peasantry organized at the household level[13] was likely found in the Hama region also.

The Hama law court registers' principal concern regarding rural areas in the eighteenth century is elites' claims to surpluses and revenues through tax farming. At the turn of the nineteenth century Hama's rural hinterland was grouped into five taxation districts (*muqata'at*); into farmlands located at some remove from the built-up areas of villages and taxed in cash (*mazari' miri maqtu'*); and into predominantly grain-producing villages taxed in kind (*qaraya hasil*).[14] These were let out to tax farmers (*multazims*), who often were beys and aghas, holders of high military-administrative rank. However, *multazims* also could include men of civil rank (efendis). *Multazims* had fiscal rights and responsibilities vis-à-vis their tax farms, which

12 LCR Hama 42:281, doc. 577, 23 Rabi' I 1140/ 8 Nov. 1727; 46:56, doc. 136, 9 Jumada II 1202/ 17 March 1788; 46:226, doc. 502, 11 Muharram 1210/ 28 July 1795. During the defense of Acre against Napoleon Bonaparte in 1799, the Hama district was ordered to send barley for provisioning troops. LCR Hama 46:360, doc. 652, 28 Safar 1214/ 1 Aug. 1799.

13 Huri Islamoglu-Inan, *State and Peasant in the Ottoman Empire: Agrarian Power Relations and Regional Economic Development in Ottoman Anatolia during the Sixteenth Century* (Leiden, 1994), 8, 13, 244.

14 LCR Hama 46:376, doc. 672, *awasit* Ramadan 1214/ 10 Feb. 1800; Dick Douwes and Norman N. Lewis, "Taxation and Agriculture in the District of Hama, 1800–1831: New Material from the Records of the Religious Court," in *The Syrian Land in the 18th and 19th Century*, ed. Thomas Philipp (Stuttgart, 1992), 263. The five rural *muqata'as* in 1800 were Hisn al-Akrad, Hazur, Masyaf, Kafrun, and Kalbiyya.

they could transfer or sublet to other tax farmers. Certain taxes were denominated in kind, others in specie.[15]

Aghas formed a significant group among the *multazims*. Aghas were responsible for ensuring rural security and collecting taxes,[16] and agha families established a hereditary presence in some areas. (The ʻAzms, as noted previously, were the most eminent of the hereditary military families to emerge from the Hama region.) The administrative hinterland of eighteenth-century Hama included a number of fortresses whose maintenance was the responsibility of the Hama government, including Salamiyya to the southeast, Masyaf to the west, and al-Hisn to the southwest.[17] Aghas exercised their fiscal functions in tandem with their military roles, as demonstrated by the commander of the Hisn garrison who also was a *multazim* for the Hisn *muqataʻa*.[18] In the mid-eighteenth century the garrison commander shared the *muqataʻa* with three other tax farmers: his brother, like the commander an agha; a Muslim from the coastal town of Jabla; and a Christian luminary named Dib. They pledged to remit revenues to Asʻad Bey al-ʻAzm (at that time the district governor of Hama) and Sulayman Pasha al-ʻAzm of Damascus, to whom the *muqataʻa* of al-Hisn was subordinate. The document mentions the fiscal/solar year (*sana martiyya*) in which the taxes were due and the amount that the *multazims* collectively owed. Three-quarters of the pledged revenues were linked to silk cultivation, and the remainder were derived from cultivation of winter grains.

The varied identities of Hisn *multazims* demonstrates that in addition to the military elites of aghas and beys, urban people of non-military status also had access to the countryside through remission of

---

15 Cf. LCR Hama 46:56, doc. 136, 9 Jumada II 1202/ 17 March 1788; and 46:355, doc. 645, 5 Shaʻban 1213/ 12 Jan. 1799; Douwes and Lewis, "Taxation and Agriculture," 263–266.

16 E.g. the agha from Aleppo who was active in the district of Ariha between Hama and Aleppo in the early 1730s. The villagers knew him simply as ʻal-Qassamʼ (in this context, ʻthe tax collectorʼ). LCR Hama 42:351, doc. 718, 25 Muharram 1145/ 18 July 1732.

17 LCR Hama 42:362, docs. 736–737, *awasit* Safar 1145/ 7 Aug. 1732; 42:384, doc. 766, 15 Shawwal 1145/ 31 March 1733.

18 LCR Hama 42:414, doc. 819, *awasit* Dhu al-Hijja 1146/ 19 May 1734.

taxes or other means. The Dib family remained tax farmers in al-Hisn for many decades, demonstrating the existence of tax-farming 'dynasties' among some district families.[19] In Hama, *multazims* from two non-military groups stand out in particular: Muslim notables and well-connected local Christians. The former included members of the 'Alwani and Kaylani families,[20] while an example of the latter is al-Mu'allim Musa walad Hanna Na'ma, scion of a family who served the local administration as scribes, clerks and accountants.[21] It is significant, though, that by the first part of the twentieth century the word 'agha' had become synonymous with landlord, underscoring the close identification of an originally military status group with claims to the land and its revenue.[22]

Taxation and cultivation rights were sometimes transferred to Hama residents by legally recognized representatives of rural people, viz., Turcoman tribal heads or Nusayri district chiefs (*muqaddams*) representing 'the people' (*ahali*) of a district.[23] Recognized tribal heads were part of the *muqata'a* system in the countryside of Hama in the eighteenth century. The Ottomans had settled Turcomans in the region as early as the sixteenth century to function as militia to deter bedouin attacks on settled areas.[24] The authorities conferred *muqata'as* of villages, including the right to cultivate the land, on Turcoman tribal groups (sing. *'ashira*) through their stewards (sing. *katkhuda*) and other 'notables' (*ikhtiyariyya*). The tribal groups' right of usufruct (*haqq al-tasarruf* [...] *min zira'a wa-ujur wa-ghayr dhalik*) was hereditary and confirmed by official deeds (sing. *sanad*).

---

19 Burckhardt, *Travels*, 159.

20 LCR Hama 46:152, doc. 316, 5 Rabi' I 1208/ 11 Oct. 1793; 46:204a, doc. 464, 1 Rajab 1209/ 22 Jan. 1795.

21 LCR Hama 46:120, docs. 248–250, 15 Muharram 1208/ 23 Aug. 1793.

22 Jacques Weulersse, *Le Pays des Alaouites* (Tours, 1940), 223.

23 E.g. LCR Hama 46:120, doc. 250, 15 Muharram 1208/ 23 Aug. 1793; 46:155, doc. 325, 21 Rabi' I 1208/ 27 Oct. 1793.

24 Rafeq, "Mazahir iqtisadiyya," 18; Weulersse, *Alaouites*, 66; Mahmud 'Umar al-Siba'i and Na'im Salim al-Zahrawi, *Hims: Dirasa Watha'iqiyya fi al-hiqba min 1256–1337 h./ 1840–1918 m.* (Homs, 1992) 13. In the latter instance, Turcomans were settled within the walls of Homs adjoining a gate that the Ottoman conqueror of Syria, Sultan Salim, had ordered sealed for security purposes.

Tribal representatives were permitted to let out the land in renewable three-year contracts, subject to judicial oversight linked to the land's *miri* tax status.[25] Subletting occurred when the tribe or others responsible for paying the taxes were unable to meet their obligations,[26] or in order to revive ruined villages and abandoned land.[27] As for *muqaddams*, they were Nusayri rural chieftains (village and clan notables) acknowledged by the Ottomans as representatives of their particular communities.[28]

The Nusayris – known today as 'Alawis – represent an offshoot of Shi'i Islam. They have had a distinct religious identity since at least the tenth century. The Nusayri faith was an esoteric one whose doctrines were fully known only to the highest ranking religious shaykhs. Rituals centered around saints' tombs, themselves often associated with prominent natural features such as springs and sacred groves. Nusayri belief and practice represented a complex synthesis of Syrian history and traditions, from pre-Christian through Christian and Islamic times. Sociologically the Nusayri identity served as a marker or boundary distinguishing this segmented and tribally organized mountain community from their neighbors and from metropolitan authority (cf. the Druze of Mount Lebanon).[29]

---

25 LCR Hama 46:105, doc. 206, 1 Rajab 1205/ 6 March 1791; 46:155, doc. 325, 21 Rabi' I 1208/ 27 Oct. 1793; 46:204a, doc. 464, 1 Rajab 1209/ 22 Jan. 1795.

26 LCR Hama 46:155, doc. 325, 21 R1 1208/ 27 Oct. 1793. For the village in question, 'Basirin and its dependencies (*tawabi'uha*)' including Kafr Hamim, the *katkhuda* and notables of the Buzuliyya Turcomans certified their inability to pay the *miri* tax or to administer and cultivate the lands properly.

27 E.g. the six-year lease of al-Butila village by its Turcoman *multazims* to lessees who were permitted to retain whatever they built by way of improvements and reconstruction; LCR Hama 46:204a, doc. 464, 1 Rajab 1209/ 22 January 1795.

28 Dick Douwes, "Knowledge and Oppression: The Nusayriyya in the Late Ottoman Period," in *La Shia Nell'Impero Ottomano* (Rome, 1993), 153–154. See also Weulersse, *Alaouites*, 333.

29 Fuad I. Khuri, "The Alawis of Syria: Religious Ideology and Organization," in *Syria: Society, Culture, and Polity*, ed. Richard T. Antoun and Donald Quataert (Albany, 1991), 49–61 *passim*; Weulersse, *Alaouites*, 51–59, 254–265.

Like the Druze, Nusayris remained largely independent of state authority, paying tribute when they were compelled to but rarely submitting to direct rule from Cairo, Damascus, or Istanbul. The Ottoman state gave no formal recognition to the Nusayris as a religious community – such recognition was reserved for Sunni Muslims, Christians, and Jews – but the state did afford Nusayris de facto political recognition by dealing with their villages through *muqaddams* representing local populations. In ideological terms, however, Ottoman-backed Sunni muftis and polemicists were fiercely antagonistic to 'heretical' Nusayri doctrines,[30] a hostility which provided ample ideological ammunition to justify Ottoman military campaigns against recalcitrant Nusayri chieftains and districts in pursuit of the government's political or fiscal interests.

Hama's eighteenth-century court records underscore the significant degree of notable and elite influence in the countryside through the system of tax farming, including the leasing out of *miri* fiscal and cultivation rights. The land system in Hama district in the eighteenth century was a hybrid, mixing classical patrimonial norms and practices with a functional devolution of wealth, influence and power to local elites and notables. The patrimonial model has been described and analyzed through case-studies of Anatolia in the sixteenth and seventeenth centuries.[31] These studies' generalizations about Ottoman ideology and practice are relevant to the district of Hama in the eighteenth century. The Ottoman state exercised its authority and collected taxes through intermediaries and officials who depended on the state for their positions and legitimacy. The intermediaries' dependence on the state was underscored by their frequent reassignment and by the state's practice of confiscating their prop-

---

30 E.g. al-Shaykh Muhammad al-Maghribi of Latakia (d. 1828). Douwes, "Knowledge and Oppression," 164–165. That Ottoman attitudes toward Nusayris were pragmatically shaped by political, not doctrinal, considerations is persuasively argued in Stefan Winter, "The Nusayris before the Tanzimat in the Eyes of Ottoman Provincial Administrators," paper presented to the Syria-III conference in Erlangen, Germany, July 2000.

31 Karen Barkey, *Bandits and Bureaucrats: The Ottoman Route to State Centralization* (Ithaca, 1994), *passim*; Islamoglu-Inan, *State and Peasant*, *passim*.

erties when they fell out of favor. Through the mechanism of the *shari'a* law courts (or *kadı* courts in the Anatolian context), the state offered peasants and cultivators a means to protest against illegal or unjust exactions on the part of its intermediaries and tax collectors. In this way, the argument continues, the formation of dyadic patron-client relationships was discouraged, and provincial intermediaries and peasants alike looked to the central authority for the advancement of their personal or collective interests.

In eighteenth-century Syria the governor or pasha was charged with this supervisory role. Governors of Damascus continued to invoke the patrimonial ideal to chastise tax collectors and officials for their unjust or illegal practices. A circular of 1788 warned village shaykhs in the Hama district not to take more than their legal share from cultivators, and denounced tax collectors (*qassamin*) who used 'fear and terror' to intimidate peasants into paying illegal taxes.[32] These themes were picked up twelve years later in another circular that emphasized the duty of officials to act with justice and mercy toward cultivators and the subject population generally, in the context of an order to reduce the rate of taxation for *hasil* villages.[33] Also consistent with the patrimonial model was the state's continued confiscation of the property of office-holders who fell out of favor (even if only temporarily), including members of provincial elites such as As'ad Bey (later Pasha) al-'Azm.[34]

Yet alongside this evidence of classical-style patrimonialism are indications of 'the rise of local power [centers] that characterized the post-sixteenth century history of the Ottoman Empire.'[35] The process of elite and notable entrenchment was discernible in eighteenth-century Hama, preceding and preparing the way for the full-blown emergence of absentee large landownership in the final period of Ottoman rule. Of the four major landowning families noted by Gertrude Bell in 1907 – al-'Azm, al-Kaylani, al-Barazi and Tayfur – the first

32 LCR Hama 46:74–77, doc. 170, 15 Rabi' I 1203/14 Dec. 1788.

33 LCR Hama 46:384, doc. 689, 13 Shawwal 1214/10 March 1800.

34 LCR Hama 46:121–122, doc. 251, 25 Rabi' II 1205/1 January 1791; 46:167, doc. 353, 3 Jumada I 1208/7 Dec. 1793.

35 Islamoglu-Inan, *State and Peasant*, 246.

two were already prominent in the countryside of the eighteenth century, while the third may have shared control of *miri* villages as part of a recognized tribal leadership.[36]

Members of the Kaylani and other notable families were creditors to people living in the Hama countryside. Rural indebtedness was nothing new; in the sixteenth century, for example, peasants in the Hama countryside owed money to *za'ims* (holders of *zi'ama* tax farms) and *timariots* (i.e Ottoman provincial cavalry who received land revenues in return for their military service).[37] State-linked elites continued to be major village creditors in the eighteenth century,[38] by which time urban notables had joined them in the business of rural moneylending. For instance, in 1728 the Christian villagers of Muhrada, represented by their 'village chief' (*rayyis* [sic] *al-qariya*), owed more than 5000 piasters to al-Shaykh Husayn Efendi al-Kaylani, head of the Qadiriyya Sufi order in Hama. This debt reflected tax payments that Husayn Efendi had made on the villagers' behalf, including the *jizya* (poll-tax) assessment for which Christians were liable.[39]

Rural people's dependence on urban moneylenders persisted as a consistent feature of Hama's countryside in the first half of the nineteenth century. By the middle and later periods of the century, when an internal and international market had developed for Hama's grain, cotton, and other agricultural products,[40] moneylenders enriched themselves through their claims on rural surpluses. Muslim aghas and

36 Bell, *Syria*, 224. A law-court document of 1791 identifies the Barazi name with the leadership of a Turcoman tribal group, but the prevalent view is that the family was Kurdish in origin. I cannot explain this discrepancy. Cf. LCR Hama 46:105, doc. 206, 1 Rajab 1205/ 6 March 1791; Al-Dbiyat, "Homs et Hama," 136; Douwes, *Ottomans in Syria*, 69.

37 Abdul-Karim Rafeq, "Al-fi'at al-ijtima'iyya wa-milkiyyat al-ard fi bilad al-Sham fi al-rub' al-akhir min al-qarn al-sadis 'ashar," *Dirasat Tarikhiyya* nos. 35–36 (March–June 1990), 120–122. *Zi'amas* were large fiscal units that subsumed a number of smaller tax farms into one regional bloc.

38 E.g. LCR Hama 42:336, doc. 685 [pt. 2], 9 Dhu al-Hijja 1144/ 3 June 1732; 42:350, docs. 716–717, 25 Muharram 1145/ 18 July 1832.

39 LCR Hama 42:294, doc. 597, *awakhir* Shawwal 1140/ 8 June 1728.

40 Guys, *Esquisse*, 220; AE, CC, Damas 3, B. de Gouy, 29 April 1853; CC, Damas 4, Hecquard, 16 Oct. 1862; France, *Bulletin consulaire français* (1885): 570–571.

'ulama' as well as wealthy Christians were among those to whom villagers owed debts. Creditors' efforts to collect individual and collective debts through the *shari'a* law court left a record for posterity. For instance, in 1852 Hamud Agha al-Jijakli, whose family had risen to prominence in the preceding decades, sued two individuals from al-Bishnin village, including the village shaykh, for a total of nearly 3000 piasters and three *shunbuls* (measures) of wheat. The major part of the debt, Hamud Agha maintained, was collectively pledged, making the village shaykh and his associate legally responsible for it. At the time the debt was incurred, the villagers had collectively pledged to make good the entire amount.[41] Collective debt brokered by village shaykhs was a recurring pattern in the mid-nineteenth century.[42] As the cash-hungry Ottoman state approached and then fell into bankruptcy, its cultivators had to come up with specie for taxes. Therefore, moneylending urban patrons became essential to the village economy, especially in the uncertain frontier of the steppe.[43]

The local government administration was keenly interested in the registration and collection of debts. For instance, in 1851 the *shari'a* court convened in the presence of the district governor and of Hama's recently established advisory council (*majlis shura*) to notarize a debt in kind owed to the notable Muhammad 'Ali Efendi al-Kaylani by the villagers of al-Yafur al-Gharbiyya. Muhammad 'Ali Efendi, like his Kaylani predecessor 100 years before, was the head of the Qadiriyya order.[44] The importance that the *majlis shura* – convened by the *mutasallim* and composed of local notables and elites[45] – placed on this debt is evidenced by the fact that its members personally witnessed the proceedings. Other evidence that the *shari'a* court acted as

---

41 LCR Hama 53:269, 10 Shawwal 1268/ 28 July 1852; 53:284, 11 Dhu al-Qa'da 1268/ 27 Aug. 1852.

42 E.g. LCR Hama 53:52, 24 Ramadan 1266/ 3 Aug. 1850; 53:158, *ghayat* Dhu al-Hijja 1267/ 26 Oct. 1851.

43 Weulersse, *Alaouites*, 363.

44 LCR Hama 53:158, *ghayat* Dhu al-Hijja 1267/ 26 Oct. 1851.

45 The *majlis shura* included men from these and other families: al-Kaylani, al-'Azm, al-'Alwani, Tayfur. LCR Hama 53:158–159, *ghayat* Dhu al-Hijja 1267/ 26 Oct. 1851; 53:197, 1 Rabi' I 1268/ 25 Dec. 1851.

an arm of the local elite and notability vis-à-vis rural people is shown in one villager's testimony that he owed Bakir Agha al-Barazi (of the ascendant landowning family) a significant cash debt (3000 piasters) that he was obliged to repay.[46] Indeed, the sums owed by rural people to urban moneylenders could be mind boggling. In a case witnessed by two highly placed Kaylanis, including Muhammad 'Ali the head of the Qadiriyya order, two Nusayri *muqaddams* acknowledged a combined debt of 160,000 piasters to a pair of creditors including a Christian from Homs. The *muqaddams* incurred this debt as guarantors (sing. *kafil*) of their 'tribe' *('ashira)*.[47] This document reveals the extent to which some of the tribally organized Nusayri peasants were in the grip of urban moneylenders even before the military subjugation of the central and northern Nusayri mountains in the latter part of the nineteenth century. The unidentified 'tribe' or community whom the *muqaddams* represented belonged to the southern section of the Nusayri peasantry who had long been subject to urban authority.[48]

This is not to say that urban creditors always got their way in debt cases. In some instances village notables used the court to fend off claims from their alleged urban creditors, as when a merchant unsuccessfully tried to hold a shaykh liable for the balance of a major debt.[49] But all in all, peasant indebtedness was a significant avenue through which urban notables exploited the countryside and gained access to the land and its resources. Villagers on the plains typically labored as sharecroppers, and many small proprietors fell into the sharecroppers' ranks when they lost their land on account of unpaid debts.[50]

The notable families of al-'Alwani and al-Kaylani also controlled rural resources through family *waqf* institutions. In the eighteenth century these endowments' major holdings were commercial properties (shops, workshops, and mills), with less emphasis on agricul-

---

46 LCR Hama 53:88, *awakhir* Dhu al-Hijja 1266/ 5 Nov. 1850.

47 LCR Hama 53:268, 10 Shawwal 1268/ 28 July 1852.

48 AE, CC, Damas 6, Gilbert, 14 Sept. 1879; NS Turquie 105, P. Bambino (Beyrouth), 20 Nov. 1897.

49 LCR Hama 53:52, 24 Ramadan 1266/ 3 Aug. 1850.

50 Weulersse, *Alaouites*, 363.

tural land.[51] The previously mentioned *waqf* of ‘Abd al-Qadir al-Kaylani (d. 1157/1744–1745) was among the biggest, and it included an agricultural estate in the Ghuta of Damascus.[52] Smaller urban-family *awqaf* possessed orchards and gardens in the vicinity of Hama.[53] These *waqf* lands were cultivated by tenants (sing. *bustani* or *musta'jir*) who paid a lease to the *waqf*, similar to the arrangement found on private freehold land. For instance, within one month of buying a *bustan* in the garden district of Zawr al-Khamsa from the mufti Muhammad Hasan al-Kaylani in 1733, ‘Abdallah al-‘Alwani put it plus many of his urban residential and commercial properties into a family *waqf*. At the time of its conversion to *waqf* the orchard (*bustan*) was being worked by a tenant, Sulayman b. Hamud al-Hilu, who paid rent to whoever owned the property.[54]

Despite the indubitable presence of *waqf* landholdings, however, their extent in the Hama region is uncertain. Evidence of agricultural *awqaf* is curiously lacking in a mid-nineteenth-century volume (no. 53) of Hama's *shari‘a* court registers, an omission all the more striking when contrasted with Damascene court material from the same period. In the hinterland of Damascus numerous villages and lands formed parts of imperial and family endowments whose existence was noted in the court registers.[55] An explanation for the scarcity of agricultural endowments in Hama's mid-nineteenth-century court records may lie in a combination of ‘privatization’ of *waqf* land[56] and Hama's status as a small district town, whose imperial *awqaf* were less extensive than those of Damascus.[57]

---

51 LCR Hama 42:397–400, doc. 795, *muntasif* Muharram 1146/ 28 June 1733; 46:251–253, doc. 541, 13 Dhu al-Qa‘da 1209/ 1 June 1795; 46:381, doc. 682, 6 Sha‘ban 1214/ 4 Jan. 1800.

52 LCR Hama 46:257, doc. 544, 25 Dhu al-Qa‘da 1211/ 22 May 1797.

53 LCR Hama 42:407, doc. 807, *awasit* Jumada I 1146/ 24 Oct. 1733; 42:414–415, doc. 820, *awakhir* Dhu al-Hijja 1146/ 2 June 1734.

54 LCR Hama 42:394, doc. 790, 8 Dhu al-Hijja 1145/ 22 May 1733; 42:397–400, doc. 795, *muntasif* Muharram 1146/ 28 June 1733.

55 Examples are cited in Reilly, “Urban Hegemony,” 455–470.

56 E.g. the numerous instances cited in al-Sabuni, *Tarikh Hamah*, 108–109.

57 Hama had nothing comparable to the Damascene *awqaf* founded by the sixteenth-century Ottoman pashas Sinan, Murad, and La La Mustafa; or

Alongside *waqf* and *miri* land there was the sphere of formally recognized legal freehold property – known as *milk* or *mulk* – through which urban people owned and traded in agricultural properties in Hama's irrigated hinterland.[58] Freehold properties included lands requiring personal care, irrigation, and intensive cultivation such as orchards and market-gardens, particularly those watered by the Orontes river. Such properties were orchards (sing. *bustan*), market-gardens (sing. *junayna*) and vineyards (sing. *karm*), which produced a variety of fruits and vegetables.[59] In fact all irrigation in the mid-Orontes region (including Hama) supported garden cultivation, while the surrounding plateau and steppe regions relied on rainfall for grain cultivation. The irrigated gardens were dominated by walnuts, apricots, almonds, vines and figs. Legumes and vegetables were grown amongst the trees.[60]

Unlike *miri-muqata'a* dry farming lands, irrigated properties were individually demarcated and were not treated merely as fragments of taxation districts or villages. As they did with *waqf*-administered properties, urban-based owners let out freehold garden properties to tenants who worked them. Examples of this relationship from the mid-eighteenth century include orchards owned by 'ulama' and *ashraf* such as 'Abd al-Qadir al-Kaylani, 'Abdallah al-'Alwani and the mufti, Muhammad Hasan al-Kaylani.[61] Patronage and debt, features of the dry farming economy, also characterized relations between notable urban landowners and *bustani*-tenants in the nineteenth century. In one example from 1851, a gardener described as the 'agent' of urban notable Muhammad Darwish al-Kaylani registered

---

indeed to the Khalid b. al-Walid *waqf* of Homs. See Ibsirli, "Preliminary Study," 121; and al-Sabuni, *Tarikh Hamah*, 108–109, 113–114.

58 E.g. Zawr al-Khamsa in LCR Hama 42:281, doc. 578, *awasit* Rabi' II 1140/ 30 Nov. 1727.

59 Specific fruits and vegetables were denoted for revenue purposes in LCR Hama 46:117, doc. 242, 13 Safar 1206/ 12 Oct. 1792.

60 Weulersse, *L'Oronte*, 57.

61 LCR Hama 42:394, docs. 790–791, 8 Dhu al-Hijja 1145/ 22 May 1733; 42:340, docs. 696–697, *awakhir* Dhu al-Hijja 1144/ 23 June 1732.

the amount which he owed to Muhammad Darwish with respect to a harvest.[62]

Military elites (aghas and beys) had a history of accumulating significant orchard and garden properties. Evidence of such acquisition is found in an inventory of properties seized from and then restored to As'ad Bey al-'Azm in 1732,[63] and decades later in the legacy of Faris Bey al-'Azm, a resident of Hama who owned agricultural properties (gardens and farms [*mazari'*]) near Tripoli and Jabla.[64] *Bustan* tenants enjoyed a far better situation than did sharecroppers in dry farming areas. In nineteenth-century Homs, for example, *bustan* tenants had their own corporation headed by a shaykh.[65] *Bustan* tenants secured individual agreements with owners (sometimes written, but mostly oral), whereas sharecroppers (*murabi'in*) and generic 'cultivators' (*zurra'in*) labored anonymously on *mazari'* and other grain-producing lands.[66]

This last point leads to a wider issue with respect to grain-producing land in Syria. Where intensive cultivation occurred, individual cultivators' rights to property were firmly established by customary or *shari'a* law. This was the case in areas of irrigated market-garden agriculture or fruit tree cultivation such as occurred in the Ghuta of Damascus, the gardens of Homs, or near Hama along the Orontes and in the western mountain foothills. In such regions it was common to find minutely subdivided individual landholdings. Cultivators could bargain for better terms, since owners needed their skilled and devoted labor to nurture trees and vines. In this manner *bustan* tenants often gained partial ownership of plantations in return for improving and caring for the land.[67] An illustration is found in the record of an unsuccessful lawsuit brought by a Hama noblewoman in

62 LCR Hama 53:148, 15 Dhu al-Hijja 1267/ 11 Oct. 1851.

63 LCR Hama 42:328–329, doc. 665, *awasit* Shawwal 1144/ 11 April 1732.

64 LCR Hama 46:207–208, doc. 457–458 [part 1], *awasit* Dhu al-Hijja 1208/ 14 July 1794.

65 Siba'i and Zahrawi, *Hims*, 78.

66 LCR Hama 46:69, doc. 164, btwn. 6–9 Muharram 1203/ 7–10 Oct. 1788; 46:207–208, doc. 457–458 [pt. 1], *awasit* Dhu al-Hijja 1208/ 14 July 1794; Weulersse, *Alaouites*, 225–226.

67 Weulersse, *Alaouites*, 224.

1849 for the return of properties that had belonged to her father in the village of al-Hawwash in the hills around al-Hisn, southwest of Hama. Her bid failed because her father had sold the unimproved property to cultivators and/or ceded ownership of part of it to cultivators in return for their planting and caring for trees.[68] But in the dry-farming, grain-growing lands of the steppe, the concept of individual cultivators' rights had little meaning. Groups of cultivators dependent on the tax farmers or landholders for security (and often for seed-grains as well) were collectively bound to surrender a portion of this harvest in return for working the land. As settlement and grain cultivation spread in the nineteenth century, so did the geographic scope of the landed estates that characterized Hama in the eyes of twentieth-century writers.[69]

The legal documentation from Hama regarding agricultural lands reveals a marked elitist and ruling-class bias. The names of villages, lands and individuals were inscribed in the Hama registers to protect the fiscal interests of the treasury and the personal interests of the elites and notables who had claims to crops, revenues, debts, and villages. The registers offer information principally on those aspects of the rural economy and society that were of particular concern to the Ottoman state, its local elites, and the notables that clustered about state institutions. Propertied but non-notable townspeople, prominent in the affairs of Damascus's Ghuta, scarcely appear in Hama documents pertaining to rural areas. Likewise Hama-region peasants are underrepresented compared with their Damascus counterparts. Even though peasants have but a minority voice in the records of Damascus courts, they nonetheless are heard there.[70] But in Hama ordinary villagers rarely used the law court to assert or defend their interests.

The few exceptions prove the rule, and they all date from the nineteenth century when government was becoming more intrusive in the life of the countryside and more difficult to evade or avoid – through its implementation of military conscription, for example.[71] In

---

68 LCR Hama 53:13, Muharram 1266/Nov.–Dec. 1849.

69 Notably Weulersse, *Alaouites*, 218–219.

70 Reilly, "Status Groups and Propertyholding," *passim*.

71 E.g. the announcement in 1850 of military conscription quotas for Homs, Hama and their surrounding districts on the basis of a recently concluded

some instances when issues could not be resolved locally villagers sued one another over contested land, livestock, or water rights.[72] Likewise, if a villager had a dispute with a person from another social category (for instance, a soldier or a bedouin), the *shari'a* court was one venue for pursuing the matter.[73] In other instances groups of villagers might register property transactions occurring among themselves.[74] Occasionally a peasant scored a legal victory over his supposed betters, as when a woman from the al-'Alwani family unsuccessfully sued a (Christian) villager over rights to a silk-producing mulberry orchard.[75] In this case the urban plaintiff took the villager to court, but his vigorous defense of his position marks a rare recorded instance when a villager in the Hama district used the judicial institution to his advantage.

Not surprisingly, shaykhs were less reticent than ordinary villagers about using the *shari'a* court. As men of standing and relative wealth who mediated between villagers and state authority, village shaykhs occasionally had compelling reasons to bring legal issues before the judge in Hama. In the mid-nineteenth century shaykhs attended the court to adjudicate disputes over debts and property, or even (as in one case) to silence defamatory gossip about a female relative.[76] Of the few rural people whose names appear in the Hama registers surveyed, only one was female: a woman from Ba'rin seeking to buy her way out of marriage (a *khul'* divorce).[77] Therefore, to

---

census of eligible males. LCR Hama 53:110–111, 5 & 17 Safar 1267/ 10 & 22 Dec. 1850.

72 LCR Hama 53:62, 24 Shawwal 1266/ 2 Sept. 1850; 53:73, 13 Dhu al-Qa'da 1266/ 20 Sept. 1850; 53:290, 1 Dhu al-Hijja 1268; 53:263, 10 Ramadan 1268/ 28 June 1852.

73 E.g. LCR Hama 53:9, 13 Dhu al-Hijja 1265/ 30 Oct. 1849; 53:137, 7 Jumada I 1267/ 10 March 1851.

74 E.g. LCR Hama 53:108, 15 Safar 1267/ 20 Dec. 1850.

75 LCR Hama 53:13, n.d. Muharram 1266/ Nov.–Dec. 1849.

76 LCR Hama 53:159, *ghayat* Dhu al-Hijja 1267/ 26 Oct. 1851; 53:245, 23 Rajab 1268/ 13 May 1852; 53:285, 15 Dhu al-Qa'da 1268/ 31 Aug. 1852; 53: 269, 11 Shawwal 1268/ 29 July 1852; 53:302, 3 Muharram 1269/ 17 Oct. 1852.

77 LCR Hama 53:98, 24 Muharram 1267/ 29 Nov. 1850. The *khul'* procedure enabled a woman to obtain a divorce (with her husband's consent) at the cost of forgoing a portion of the brideswealth that would otherwise by owed her by

the slight degree that village property matters were adjudicated in the Hama court, women were unrepresented. Again, their absence in Hama differs from the pattern observed in nineteenth-century Damascus, where women's legal claims to agricultural properties were explicitly and frequently documented.

The absence of ordinary villagers from the Hama documentation merits examination. In Hama proper, ordinary people – *ra'aya* – frequently used the courts to adjudicate disputes or to deal with questions of urban life, whereas Hama's peasants were judicially (and judiciously?) silent. But in an earlier century the Hama court reportedly had enjoyed a reputation for defending peasants against unjust officials.[78] The Islamic law court's role as a channel for the expression of peasant grievances has been identified as an important characteristic of the classical patrimonial system.[79] Hama may already, as early as the mid-eighteenth century, have taken on an aura of opposition to its hinterland and begun to be regarded as a bastion of urban privilege that was unaccommodating to the poorer peasants and villagers.[80] In an urban context notables and elites including the Kaylanis and 'Azms might aspire to present themselves (in patrimonial fashion) as patrons, protectors, and guarantors of justice;[81] but in the hinterland they and the urban institutions they represented were viewed in a more suspect light. Douwes's study of Ottoman provincial administration in Syria speaks of the institutionalization of oppression

---

her husband. See Judith E. Tucker, *In the House of the Law: Gender and Islamic Law in Ottoman Syria and Palestine* (Berkeley, 1998), 95–100.

78 Barghuth, "Liwa' Hamah," 86.

79 Barkey, *Bandits and Bureaucrats*, 39, 107; Islamoglu-Inan, *State and Peasant*, 7.

80 On this reputation see Al-Dbiyat, "Homs et Hama," 34, 140.

81 For instance when Isma'il Bey (later Pasha) al-'Azm was district governor of Homs, Hama, and Ma'arra in the early eighteenth century, he made a point of distributing foodstuffs for the poor and needy. The Kaylanis, as already noted, were judges, jurisconsults, and Sufis, and in these functions they represented *shar'i* legitimacy and Qadiriyya spirituality. As'ad, *Tarikh Hims*, 2:342–344; James A. Reilly, "Ottoman Authority and Local Society in Late Eighteenth-Century Hama," *Arab Historical Review for Ottoman Studies* nos. 13–14 (October 1996), 131–134; cf. al-Makki, *Tarikh Hims*, 60–61, 97, 140, 144, 203, 218, 123, 225.

in the countryside: 'By the late 18th century injustice had long since become a natural companion of the provincial administration.'[82] There was a logic to this practice. By giving local officials nearly free rein over the peasants the central government did not have to bear the full costs of administration; while at the same time officials' inevitable 'transgressions' made them vulnerable to politically expedient interventions from the center in the name of restoring justice. Against these benefits of oppression, the Ottoman center had to weigh the costs, including reduced productivity and abandonment of villages.[83] The endemic abuse of authority by aghas and other rural tax collectors,[84] and their use of 'fear and terror' (in the Damascus governor's words), help to explain the reluctance of villagers to expose themselves to the alien authority that the *shari'a* court represented. These urban–rural differences were often accentuated by confessional ones, particularly in the rural *muqata'as* where Nusayris were a majority of the population. As a rule peasants preferred to settle their differences outside the framework of the urban *shari'a* court.[85]

The contempt harbored by some among the elite for Nusayri peasants is evident in an incident that occurred near Homs in 1795, when a Turcoman agha reportedly yoked two Nusayri villagers and used them as draught animals.[86] The extension of cultivation in the plains, combined with population pressure in the 'Alawi mountains, compelled many poor Nusayris to come down from the mountains in the nineteenth century and work the lands of urban proprietors in the Homs and Hama districts. Conditions in the plains villages were difficult in any case due to the villages' exposure to raids and to robbery, and their dependence on fickle winter rains. The lives of Nusayri peasants on the plains was hardest of all since these newcomers were

---

82 Douwes, "Justice and Oppression," 63.

83 Douwes, *Ottomans in Syria*, chap. 7.

84 See, e.g. LCR Hama 46:74–77, doc. 170, 15 Rabi' I 1203/ 14 Dec. 1788; Anon., *Journey*, 28; Volney, *Travels*, 2:297; Lyde, *Ansyreeh*, 44–48; Douwes and Lewis, "Taxation and Agriculture," 268–271.

85 Doumani notes a similar phenomenon in Jabal Nablus, where confessional differences were not an issue and where customary law prevailed in rural areas for the most part. Doumani, *Rediscovering Palestine*, 28.

86 As'ad, *Tarikh Hims*, 2:363.

deprived of the political protection that *muqaddams* provided their co-religionists in the mountain and hill districts.[87]

While the creation of large landed estates in the region of Hama during the nineteenth century has not yet been subject to an archives-based study, the general outlines of this process have been sketched. Mohamad Al-Dbiyat writes that after the Ottoman reconquest of Syria from the Egyptian army of Ibrahim Pasha in 1840, the Ottomans exempted from taxes and military service subjects who settled and founded new villages east of the Orontes. Nusayris and Isma'ilis from the coastal mountains, sedentarized bedouins, and immigrants and refugees (including Circassians) settled the steppes, while urban elites and notables gained ownership of these estates through the mechanism of the Ottoman land code promulgated in 1858. In addition, prominent Hamawis received land grants from the sultan in recognition of their service; purchased villages from tribal chiefs who (Al-Dbiyat alleges) 'had little attachment to the land,' or perhaps did not appreciate the full significance of the transactions to which they agreed; and obtained land from indebted peasants unable to repay loans. The upshot of all this was that sharecropping became the predominant form of cultivation on the newly settled steppes. Sharecroppers came to regard Hama as a bastion of 'feudalists' remembered later for their 'voracity and tyranny.'[88] Another modern study has said of Hama:

> the great families who had links to the Ottoman administration acquired urban and rural properties by various means and to such an extent that it was rare to find properties or land possessed by ordinary individuals among the people.[89]

This statement reflects a common view of the general situation as it existed in the Hama district in the later Ottoman and Mandate periods. Archives that document this process have yet to be identified and studied, however. Since the land records of the Syrian government are

87 Weulersse, *Alaouites*, 60, 336, 364, 370–372.

88 Al-Dbiyat, "Homs et Hama," 30, 137, 144.

89 Musa and Harba, *Muhafazat Hamah*, 89.

still not easily available to researchers,[90] future work on this question may have to focus on the Ottoman records in Istanbul.

The purpose of the Ottoman land code of 1858 was not to create private landownership, for this in large measure already existed. Rather, the code's major aim was to solidify or establish the modernizing state's claim to land revenues by making landholders accountable to the state for their title-deeds, and by emphasizing their responsibility for payment of taxes.[91] In locales where individual title and smallholdings already were long established, the 1858 code provided a new bureaucratic mechanism for representing an older situation. Such was the case in the oasis of Damascus or the villages around Jerusalem.[92] But in other regions where smallholdings or individual title were not well established (e.g. the steppes and plains of Syria and Palestine) large tracts were registered in the names of merchants, notables, or tribal shaykhs who were willing to take responsibility for revenues.[93] Titleholders' rewards included the op-

---

90 One exception, based on files in the Ministry of Agriculture and Agrarian Reform, is Ramez George Tomeh, "Landownership and Political Power in Damascus, 1858–1958" (M.A. thesis, American University of Beirut, 1977).

91 Peter Sluglett and Marion Farouk-Sluglett, "The Application of the 1858 Land Code in Greater Syria: Some Preliminary Observations," in *Land Tenure and Social Transformation in the Middle East*, ed. Tarif Khalidi (Beirut, 1984), 413–415; Quataert, "Age of Reforms," 857–860.

92 Haim Gerber, *Ottoman Rule in Jerusalem 1890–1914* (Berlin, 1985), 201, 219; Reilly, "Status Groups and Propertyholding," 528–531.

93 Contemporary accounts emphasize the consolidation of 'abandoned' Syrian and Palestinian plains lands in the hands of speculators. In Ottoman Transjordan, tribal shaykhs registered land both as a defensive measure against potential challengers, and in response to new commercial opportunities. The Transjordanian context contrasts sharply with that of the tribal regions of southern Iraq, where land deeds became political chits in a system of rewards and punishments for cooperative or obstreperous shaykhs. The land situation in the northern Iraqi province of Mosul was different yet again. Clearly the 1858 land code was far from Procrustean; rather, it was an administrative tool whose results varied according to local conditions and circumstances. Great Britain, *Parliamentary Papers* (1880), 74:247; Eugene L. Rogan, *Frontiers of the State in the Late Ottoman Empire: Transjordan, 1850–1921* (Cambridge, 1999), chap. 3; Albertine Jwaideh, "Aspects of Land Tenure and Social Change in Lower Iraq during Late Ottoman Times," in

portunity to profit from the extension of agricultural markets that characterized the nineteenth century. The plains of Hama often are cited as a classic example of the emergence of large landownership in the nineteenth-century context.[94]

Despite their limitations, the *shari'a* law-court registers help to delineate the character of urban–rural relations in the Hama district in the eighteenth and nineteenth centuries. The registers affirm that two of the modern landowning families (al-'Azm and al-Kaylani) were already prominent in the affairs of the countryside in the eighteenth century as tax farmers, creditors, and/or *waqf* administrators. The other two families – Barazi and Tayfur – were relative latecomers who owed their emergence to their links to the Ottoman military and to tribal elites. Unlike the military family of the 'Azms, however, the Barazis and Tayfurs remained Hama-based and did not extend their influence to Damascus or other centers. The Barazis had, however, established themselves as the town's leading landowning family by the period of the French Mandate. In the 1930s, they owned 49 villages in Hama's hinterland, compared to 25 for the 'Azms and 24 for the Kaylanis.[95]

An additional point that emerges from the *shari'a* registers, as much by inference as by direct evidence, is the dissociation or alienation of the rural hinterland from the city. With the few exceptions noted in this chapter, the ordering and structuring of village life occurred independently of the urban-based judicial system, and Hama-area peasants showed little inclination to use the court system. A possible explanation of the peasants' silence or absence is that they saw the *shari'a* court as representative of urban and propertied interests rather than of their own. This alienation, rooted in the objective opposition of rural and urban interests, was further deepened by the existence of confessional differences between town and country. (The reference here is to the Nusayris, who as a 'heretical'

Land Tenure and Social Transformation in the Middle East, ed. Tarif Khalidi (Beirut, 1984), 333–351; Sarah D. Shields, *Mosul before Iraq: Like Bees Making Five-Sided Cells* (Albany, 2000), 141–147.

94 Quataert, "Age of Reforms," 863.

95 Weulersse, *Alaouites*, 362–363.

community were not formally recognized by the Ottoman authorities. Urban and rural Christians, whose client [*dhimmi*] status was legally recognized, were more integrated into the *shar'i* legal system.) Thus the *shari'a* court registers offer insight into the historical origins of twentieth-century issues including absentee urban landholding, agitation for land reform, and the potential for intertwined political and confessional tensions in the Hama district.

Once more, Hama appears as a kind of microcosm for wider Syrian developments. The consolidation of absentee landholding in its hinterland illustrates what Philip S. Khoury has identified as the rise of a dominant 'bureaucratic-landholding' class in Ottoman Syria from the second half of the nineteenth century onward.[96] Given the modest size of their town and political base, Hama's notables were politically overshadowed by their counterparts in Aleppo and especially Damascus. Nevertheless, landowning families and their descendants played significant roles in the politics of Hama until the land reforms of the 1950s.[97] Tensions in and around Hama since then have arisen not only from the dichotomies of town and country and of landlord and sharecropper, but also from the acute confessional differences that overlapped with and reinforced these other divisions.

96 Khoury, *Urban Notables*, chap. 2, *passim*.
97 Petran, *Syria*, 97.

Chapter Six: Rural–Urban Networks, Landed Estates, and the World Economy

Hama's ties to its rural hinterland had long been a feature of its economic life, but these ties took on new dimensions in the course of the nineteenth century. With the integration of Syria into the capitalist world economy, land and its produce became commodified to an unprecedented degree. At the same time Hama's textile manufactures, while remaining pre-industrial in form, also adapted to the regional and international environment that was connected to the Industrial Revolution. By the end of the Ottoman period, Hama's encounters with 'modernity' had paradoxically helped to generate its reputation as a bastion of social and economic conservatism.

The historical significance of the pastoral hinterland to denizens of Hama such as administrators and merchants, highlighted by the example of the pilgrimage caravan, was reflected in other ways as well. Townspeople and pastoralists belonging to local tribes[1] had economic ties with each other at a number of levels. In the eighteenth century, for instance, we find commercial partnerships between townspeople and bedouins. In 1797 a dyer who worked with indigo had a bedouin partner (*sharik*) in ownership of a herd of goats.[2] Another type of commercial relationship between town and steppe was the phenomenon of pastoralists and townspeople as creditors of each other. Creditor-debtor relationships and economic partnerships are helpful indices for the parameters and extent of regional

---

1 These local tribes were affiliated with the Mawali tribal confederation, and they were put under pressure by the northern migration of 'Anaza bedouin in the eighteenth century. The local tribes numbered some 25 in the early nineteenth century. See Douwes, *Ottomans in Syria*, 34–40.

2 Thirteen and a half goats, to be precise; an anatomical marvel if taken literally. The fraction probably reflects the dyer's and bedouin's share of a larger herd. LCR Hama 46:445–446, doc. 533 (pt. 1), 27 Rajab 1211/ 26 Jan. 1797.

economies in Syria, providing tools for measuring where the hinterland of one urban center tapered off and gave way to the influence of another.[3] In the pre-capitalist context of Ottoman Syria, partnerships and creditor-debtor relationships reflected personal ties of cooperation or of clientage, signaling not only economic relationships (in the modern, impersonal use of the word), but a dense network of social ties also.[4]

In a pattern reminiscent of Jabal Nablus in Ottoman Palestine,[5] creditor-debtor relationships in Hama and its hinterland reflected investment partnerships (sing. *mudaraba*) or speculative futures contracts (sing. *salam*). *Mudaraba* investment partnerships, generically known as *commenda*, were a venerable and widespread form of contract in Mediterranean trade.[6] *Mudaraba* or *commenda*'s basic principle was that owners of capital put money into enterprises worked by an active partner, with the investor sharing the risk and the profit. *Salam* speculative contracts entailed advance purchases of goods by means of which owners of capital extended credit and obtained guaranteed prices for commodities regardless of the commodities' actual market price on the date of delivery some time later.[7]

In the Hama district these transactions ranged in value from modest to quite significant. The lower end of the town–steppe creditor scale is represented by an inheritance registered in 1793 that belonged to one 'Izz al-Din b. al-Hajj A'rabi, a town-dweller. The relatively low value of his house and the absence of itemized possessions in his

---

3 Abdel-Nour, *Introduction*, 262–265; Rafeq, "Dependent Countryside," 674–677

4 Cf. Doumani, *Rediscovering Palestine*, 78–92.

5 Ibid. 166–167.

6 Abraham L. Udovitch, *Partnership and Profit in Medieval Islam* (Princeton, 1970), 171.

7 For examples of *mudaraba* and *salam* in eighteenth and nineteenth-century Hama, see the references to a deceased cloth merchant's *salam* contracts; to the 'people of capital' (*ahl rasmal al-dukkan*) who had invested in the shop of a sweets-maker; and to a silent partnership in a business deal in the village of Masyaf. LCR Hama 46:379–80; 53:72, 6 Dhu al-Qa'da 1266/ 13 Sept. 1850; 53:256, 19 Shawwal 1268/ 6 Aug. 1852.

estate indicate that ‘Izz al-Din did not live in luxury, yet well over half of his assets were loans or advances that he had made to others. His largest debtor was a bedouin of the Bani Khalid. The latter were one of the larger and wealthier local tribes in the area who enjoyed excellent relations with the people of Homs and Hama.[8] A grain dealer who died two years later, al-Hajj Mustafa b. al-Hajj Ahmad al-Sarmini, also was a bedouin's creditor.[9] A merchant with diverse interests, al-Sayyid Ahmad b. al-Sayyid Yusuf ‘Uwayda, died the same year. In addition to large quantities of soap, henna, and olive oil (demonstrating his dealings with olive-growing villages in Syria plus the Arabian caravan trade), al-Sayyid Ahmad's legacy included ownership of 75 sheep and a loan to one ‘Salih the bedouin.’[10] A wool dealer who left a sizable legacy in 1793, al-Sayyid ‘Abd al-Rahman al-Sawwaf, had intensive relationships with Hama's pastoral hinterland. His legacy included 80 head of sheep, hides, loans or credit to a number of people including two bedouins, as well as an orchard, a house, and personal items.[11] The officially recognized titular leader of the local tribes (*shaykh al-mashayikh ‘urban liwa’ Hamah*) died deeply indebted in 1850. The long list of his creditors included Muslim and Christian urban moneylenders, aghas, and other bedouins.[12]

Although most of the recorded credit flows went outward from the town to the steppe, occasionally they flowed inward when wealthy pastoralists made loans or monetary advances to associates in town. One such example is Muhammad al-Hamad al-Badawi (‘of the Iskandar Arabs’), whose legacy in 1793 included loans or credit to a number of people. None of them was clearly identified as a fellow bedouin (*‘arab*), though some may well have been. Two held the rank of bey, indicating links to the Ottoman administrative system; but because of the Ottomans' practice of conferring titles on rural strong-

---

8 LCR Hama 46:165, doc. 348, 18 Jumada I 1208/ 22 Dec. 1793. On the Bani Khalid see Zakariyya, *Asha'ir al-Sham*, 444–449.

9 LCR Hama 46:226, doc. 501, 5 Rabi‘ I 1210/ 19 Sept. 1795.

10 LCR Hama 46:216, doc. 483, 17 Shawwal 1209/ 7 May 1795.

11 LCR Hama 46:191, doc. 426 (pt. 1), 13 Jumada I 1208/ 17 Dec. 1793.

12 LCR Hama 53:79–80, 27 Dhu al-Qa‘da 1266/ 4 Oct. 1850.

men, these particular beys may not have been based in Hama itself. However, one name among Muhammad al-Hamad's debtors, Husayn al-'Alwani, was almost certainly a townsman. As already noted, the 'Alwani name was borne by a prominent family of *ashraf* and Sufis who lived on the Suq side of the river. This Husayn al-'Alwani was related in some fashion to Muhammad al-Hamad, and he approved the guardianship arrangements made by the court for the al-Hamad's minor children.[13]

Capital and credit flows from town to country and occasionally vice-versa corroborate the generalization made earlier about the importance of the pastoral hinterland to Hama's economy, including the stimulus that the relationship between town and steppe gave to the expansion of Hama along the right bank of the Orontes. More generally, close ties between townspeople and local bedouins are evident in the entire region of Homs and Hama along the middle Orontes. A documented example of this pattern is also found in Homs, where for example a wealthy bedouin shaykh owned an orchard and a home in the nineteenth century.[14]

Besides long-distance trade and trade with steppe pastoralists, Hama and its people had a multiplicity of relationships to their agricultural hinterland. Some evidence of this has already been touched on, including the role of the countryside as the provider of raw materials for the weaving industry and other crafts, and as a source of food. In a pattern reminiscent of Damascus,[15] people of Hama were closely bound up with their town's immediate hinterland of market-garden agriculture and silk-rearing villages. In contrast, Hama's links to the grain-growing lands of extensive agriculture further afield were mediated through officials and elites of military rank. Officials and

13 LCR Hama 46:154, doc. 321, 14 Rabi' I 1208/ 20 Oct. 1793.

14 al-Sib'ai and al-Zahrawi, *Hims*, 29. The shaykh in question was Majwal al-Masrab of the Saba tribe. He was known among Europeans for his marriage to the maverick English aristocrat Jane Digby, and he also possessed a house in Damascus. See Mary S. Lovell, *A Scandalous Life: The Biography of Jane Digby el Mezrab* (London, 1995). Ties between urban merchants and steppe pastoralists characterized urban life in other Ottoman districts as well, such as Mosul in northern Iraq. Shields, *Mosul before Iraq*, 164–175.

15 Reilly, "Status Groups," 517–539.

elites used their access to village harvests to engage both in licit and illicit trade.[16] Flour mills were the destination for much of the grain harvest. Found along the length of the Orontes, mills were sometimes associated with water wheels, and they used the same dams as the wheels for channeling the water and increasing its pressure. But more often mills stood alone and gave the appearance of being rudimentary structures. Appearances could be deceiving, however, since mills played a major role in the grain economy of Hama's region. Typically they were in the hands of urban elites and notables, whose control of mills was one more factor in the city's economic domination of the peasantry. For aghas and beys who dominated the provision of grain, control of mills represented a kind of vertical integration of economic assets.[17]

Mills often were dedicated to *waqf* endowments, and user-rights as well as ownership shares of *waqf* properties were commodified. In principle, rights of use and ownership were open to anyone with money. Urban notables, well-to-do villagers, and Muslims and Christians bought and sold shares of *waqf* properties. As custodians of *awqaf* or owners of mills, members of notable families were prominent stake-holders in the milling trade. In 1792, for instance, Ibrahim b. Sa'id al-Kaylani, the Hanafi mufti of Hama, and his relative 'Abd al-Razzaq b. Isma'il al-Kaylani, the *naqib al-ashraf*, consolidated their ownership shares of a mill located midway between Hama and Homs at al-Rastan. They bought their additional shares from beys, Christian villagers, and their social counterpart the mufti of Homs, 'Abd al-Hamid b. 'Abd al-Wahhab al-Siba'i.[18] A few years later the same *naqib*, 'Abd al-Razzaq, bought shares of a mill just outside of Hama (Bab Hims, adjoining the Ma'muriyya water wheel) that had belonged to his late brother Mustafa. 'Abd al-Razzaq acquired approximately one-tenth ownership of the mill, with the balance of its

---

16 See As'ad, *Tarikh Hims*, 2:342; LCR Hama 42:281, doc. 577, 23 Rabi' I 1140/ 8 Nov. 1727.

17 LCR Hama 46:173, doc. 363, 10 Rabi' I 1207/ 26 Oct. 1792; As'ad, *Tarikh Hims*, 2:344; Weulersse, *L'Oronte*, 59.

18 LCR Hama 46:172, doc. 362, 10 Rabi' I 1207/ 26 Oct. 1792; 46:173, doc. 363, 10 Rabi' I 1207/ 26 Oct. 1792; 46:173–174, doc. 364, *awasit* Rabi' I 1207/ 31 Oct. 1792.

ownership divided among a number of other people including Sulayman Efendi al-'Alwani and his mother, a daughter of Ishaq Efendi al-Kaylani.[19] The association of urban notables with mills and milling was still evident nearly 60 years later, when a subsequent *naqib al-ashraf*, Hasan Efendi al-Kaylani, and his paternal uncle 'Abd al-Rahman Efendi had a dispute with a miller regarding the amount of rent that the latter owed them.[20] Such association with milling suggests that notables shared interests with grain-trading military elites, demonstrating an economic aspect to political alliances such as that between the Kaylanis and the al-'Azms.

Prosperous Hamawis were linked to Hama's immediate environs through ownership of market-gardens, farms, and livestock. Examples from the late eighteenth century suggest that urbanites with rural interests were well-to-do individuals with a mercantile and commercial (rather than subsistence) orientation. Recall first the legacy of the wool dealer 'Abd al-Rahman al-Sawwaf (d. 1793), discussed earlier in connection with urban–steppe relations.[21] In addition to sheep, copper goods, cash, and personal effects, his legacy included the capital assets (*qima*) of an orchard (*bustan*),[22] appraised at more than the value of his house (350 and 250 piasters, respectively). The legacy of another wealthy merchant, al-Sayyid 'Uthman b. al-Sayyid Muhammad Rukiyya (d. 1792), included a large quantity of silk (worth 1,600 piasters), cattle and agricultural tools (400 piasters), one-third ownership of an opulent house (300 piasters), and a considerable number of debts payable.[23] These urban bourgeois had company in their dealings with the countryside; not surprisingly, people of military status were also engaged in the market-garden and cattle-raising economy. One example is provided by the legacy of a certain al-Hajj Muhammad Agha (d. 1788).[24] We know little about his origins except that he was the grandson of a pasha on his mother's side. (The

19 LCR Hama 46:313, doc. 600, 6 Safar 1214/ 10 July 1799.

20 LCR Hama 53:128, 17 Rabi' II 1267/ 19 Feb. 1851.

21 LCR Hama 46:191, doc. 426 (pt. 1), 13 Jumada I 1208/ 17 Dec. 1793.

22 For *qima* cf. Reilly, "Properties," *Arabica* 37 (1990): 93; Miura, "Socio-Economic Relations."

23 LCR Hama 46:129, doc. 268, 15 Rajab 1206/ 9 March 1792.

24 LCR Hama 46:66–68, doc. 161, 19 Dhu al-Qa'da 1202/ 21 Aug. 1788.

inheritance document does not even name his father.) Besides personal effects, his legacy included a group of 50 beehives (100 piasters), a watchman's house (200 piasters), 62 sheep (434 piasters), a pair (*faddan*) of oxen and crops (nominally 800 piasters, but whose appraisal was reduced to 500 since the oxen were emaciated). Finally, there is documentary evidence of a farming partnership between an urban notable, the Hanafi mufti al-Sayyid Ibrahim al-Kaylani (mentioned previously in connection with the mill at al-Rastan), and the commander of the caravansary and fortress at Shaykhun, al-Sayyid 'Abdallah Agha b. al-Sayyid Ahmad Agha. They were partners in cereal lands (a *mazra'a*) pertaining to the village of Kafr 'Ayn.[25] The document reports the amicable dissolution of the partnership, encompassing plow-oxen, unripened crops, cattle, sheep, and pack-animals. The mufti was a creditor to 'Abdallah Agha who, in addition to being the former's partner, supervised the working of the Kafr 'Ayn *mazra'a*.

Another instance of a farming partnership between an agha and Hama's notables is preserved in a legacy from 1849. It belonged to a certain 'Abd al-Qadir b. Ahmad Shawhar, and shows that he was the agent in a partnership with some members of the al-'Azm and al-Kaylani families.[26] The legacy included large amounts of silk, livestock, and cotton, but his debts were greater than his assets. His creditors included Husayn Bey al-'Azm, the wives of Muhammad Bey al-'Azm (a partner and creditor who had predeceased 'Abd al-Qadir), al-Shaykh Mustafa al-'Alwani, and others including 'Abd al-Qadir's wife. They likely were investors in 'Abd al-Qadir's business transactions via silent partnership (*mudaraba*). Although it is hard to know how common such partnerships were, their existence is signaled by their occasional registration in the court, such as one from 1852 involving two people in an unspecified business in the village of Masyaf.[27] In sum, links with food production and the countryside are leitmotifs in the economic profiles of Hama's prosperous notables, merchants, and elites.

---

25 LCR Hama 46:152, doc. 316, 5 Rabi' I 1208/ 11 Oct. 1793.

26 LCR Hama 53:11, 22 Dhu al-Hijja 1265/ 8 Nov. 1849.

27 LCR Hama 53:256, 19 Shawwal 1268/ 6 Aug. 1852.

Trade with the pastoral steppe and with other parts of the Ottoman Empire continued to characterize significant sectors of Hama's economy in the nineteenth century. From the 1830s onward, though, Hama's trade occurred in a context different from before. The older Ottoman caravan economy[28] was supplanted by and folded into a new, European-dominated world economy driven by the needs of capitalist industrialization. *Grosso modo*, the leading European powers sought to secure their access to the raw materials and the markets of the Ottoman Middle East, and to this end they strove to create new political, administrative and financial arrangements in the dwindling possessions of the Ottoman Empire. Although French interest in the Levantine cotton trade of the eighteenth century anticipated later developments, the real impact of the new world economy did not strike Syria until after the commercial disruptions of the Napoleonic Wars which ended in 1815. England's burgeoning industries, freed of their preoccupation with war production, began to flood Syrian and Ottoman markets with inexpensive, mass-produced textiles that challenged the competitive position of Syrian weavers and artisans while creating new business opportunities for Ottoman importers and re-exporters. At the same time, England's and Western Europe's demand for food and raw materials opened new vistas for Ottoman elites with access to the land and its surpluses. Existing regional and interregional economic ties within the Ottoman Fertile Crescent were reconfigured.

Even though merchants trod the same paths as before, now they did so as agents and purveyors of foreign manufactures. While many merchants continued to do well, others found themselves sidelined. Some indigenous handicrafts (especially textiles) were subjected to severe competitive pressures as craft corporations lost their ability to regulate local markets and protect their trades. Syrian manufacturers, in turn, sought to make up for lower profit margins by extending their markets. They worked to identify and appeal to popular tastes. Now

28 Masters, *Origins*, *passim*.

using imported rather than locally spun threads, merchant-manufacturers reduced artisans' wages and cheapened their low-end products, attempting to reach new clientele of villagers and bedouins. The extension and intensification of trade, both international and regional, created concomitant pressures and incentives for the improvement of communications routes. Carriage roads and railways were introduced into Syria over the course of the nineteenth century, and the advent of steamship traffic increased Syria's maritime trade many-fold. Formerly outposts of the Syrian interior, ports such as Alexandretta, Tripoli, Beirut and Jaffa took on greater importance. The Syrian-Palestinian interior and hill countries now served as population reservoirs for the rapidly expanding coastal cities and plantations.

These pressures had their first major impact on Hama during the period of Egyptian rule (1831–40). The occupation of Syria by the armies of Muhammad 'Ali Pasha and his son Ibrahim Pasha ushered in a decidedly new form of government. Not content with merely taxing the population through various intermediaries, the Egyptian regime introduced modern concepts of state, law, and sovereignty. It intervened vigorously in the processes of production, introduced military conscription, upset time-honored communal balances by advocating civic and social equality among Muslims, Christians and Jews, and for the first time in living memory brought Syria under a strong central authority that sought to redefine the role of notable and elite intermediaries. These Egyptian initiatives came in response to new conditions faced by Middle Eastern governments in the nineteenth century, as their economies and polities entered into new political and economic relationships with industrial capitalist Europe. When Ottoman authority returned to Syria in 1840, the main lines of the Egyptian initiatives were continued in Syria and other provinces of the Empire under the sobriquet of the Tanzimat, the Ottoman reform program. For many in Hama the period of Egyptian rule was particularly unhappy, and they remembered it as one of severe repression. Hama's local historian al-Sabuni, writing in the early twentieth century, asserts that Ibrahim Pasha treated people like cattle, and al-Sabuni attributed the town's depopulation to Ibrahim's harsh rule.[29]

The return of Ottoman authority in 1840 brought no immediate respite. The middle decades of the nineteenth century were marked by revolts, rebellions, uprisings, and sectarian warfare in different parts of Syria as the old Ottoman order crumbled and various sections of the population sought either to defend their time-honored privileges, to obtain new rights, or to restore a normative model of justice and order. Political violence in Aleppo, Nablus, Mount Lebanon and Damascus took on a new, inter-confessional character as their old social and political orders dissolved and broke down.[30]

Hama itself was spared civil and confessional strife. As a small district town, Hama and its population were not drawn into the same degree of ferment that characterized the situations of Aleppo, Damascus, and Mount Lebanon in this period. Hama's conflicts were principally played out in the countryside, as state authorities gradually subdued independent pastoralist and mountain peasant communities through a combination of co-optation and military force. Hama's experience in this regard was part of a larger Syrian story, suggesting parallels with the Ottomans' extended and bloody 'pacification' of the Hawran region south of Damascus from the 1860s onward.[31] Here too the Ottomans alternated between tactics of coercion and co-optation in order to subdue historically independent communities of pastoral nomads and of mountain peasants. The latter's estrangement from urban culture and power was expressed through confessional differentiation (Nusayris in the mountains west of Hama; Druze in the Hawran and Lebanon mountains).

The upshot of such 'pacification' was the transformation of Hama's pastoral hinterland into a region of extensive cultivation dominated by big landlords based in the town. Historically autonomous

---

29 al-Sabuni, *Tarikh Hamah*, 85.

30 Leila Tarazi Fawaz, *An Occasion for War: Civil Conflict in Lebanon and Damascus in 1860* (Berkeley, 1994), chap. 1; Y. Bruce Masters, "The 1850 Events in Aleppo: An Aftershock of Syria's Incorporation into the Capitalist World System," *International Journal of Middle East Studies* 22 (1990): 3–20.

31 Schilcher, "Hauran Conflicts"; Hanna, *al-Qadiyya al-Zira'iyya*, 175–184.

rural communities in the hills and mountains paid the price in terms of loss of traditional liberties. Their losses amounted to a net gain for urban interests, however. With the countryside (and its obstreperous armed residents) subdued, the volume and regularity of pilgrimage and commercial traffic increased. Regional and long-distance trade continued along the older routes, made more secure by the reformed state structure that the Ottomans built up in the second half of the nineteenth century.

The extension of security into the steppe hinterland was decisively achieved in the second half of the nineteenth century. In 1851 the route between Aleppo and Hama was still insecure for travelers. Among the highwaymen were irregular troops who drew little distinction between tax collection and robbery.[32] The steppe approaching Hama from the north was lightly populated, and its spotty cultivation contrasted sharply with the greenery of the city itself.[33] In another symptom of insecurity, the governor of Damascus warned his subordinates in 1852 of incursions into the Hama region of large numbers of 'Anaza bedouins from the east who threatened cultivators, travelers, and the collection of state revenues.[34] At about the same time, Nusayri mountain peasants to the west and northwest of Hama frequently held up and robbed travelers and caravans.

By the end of the nineteenth century, however, these types of challenges to urban-based authority had been overcome, and the government exercised unprecedented authority. Summarizing the changes that had occurred in the countryside, a French agent in Beirut with close ties to Hama noted in 1897 that the subjugation of bedouins and Nusayris in the previous 20 years had permitted agricultural, industrial, and commercial growth:

> [L]a population rurale de la province de Hama-Homs vit, à l'heure qu'il est, relativement heureuse et dans un état d'esprit fort calme [...] à aucun époque le Gouvernement n'a dominé la situation intérieure comme il la domine à l'heure

---

32 Lyde, *Ansyreeh*, 44–48.

33 Ibid. 55–56.

34 LCR Hama 53:267, 2 Shawwal 1268/ 20 July 1852.

> qu'il est et n'a exercé, avec plus d'absolutisme, son pouvoir et sur autorité [...] comme il l'a aujourd'hui [...].[35]

The cost of this security was typically paid by subjugated mountain peasants and pastoralists, many of whom henceforth lived as sharecroppers on lands belonging to their chieftains, to urban notables, or to the sultan himself.[36] But the town, dependent as it was on trade and commerce for prosperity, benefited and grew. At mid-century the districts of Homs and Hama provided about two-thirds of the grain that Tripoli exported to Europe. In addition, Hama sent soda to the soap manufactories of 'Turkey,'[37] and during the cotton boom stimulated by the American civil war Hama's merchants provided cotton for the weaving industry of Damascus.[38] By the late 1870s Hama was sending significant quantities of wool to Tripoli for export to France, over and above the wool used in Hama's local industries.[39] A decade later, Hama's cotton and silk goods were finding ready markets not only in Damascus and in Syrian coastal towns, but also in Egypt.[40] In the 1880s Homs and Hama were exporting via Tripoli wool, silk and cotton cloths, and cereals; the latter were bound for Italy.[41]

The intensification of Hama's regional and international commerce was part of a broader Syrian trend. Some of the older trade routes declined in relative or absolute terms (especially the cross-desert route to Iraq after the Suez Canal opened in 1869), but other routes grew in importance (e.g. the maritime trade with Egypt and Europe).[42] By the end of the nineteenth century Hama, like other parts of the Syrian interior, had been reoriented commercially toward the Mediterranean. The Ottoman authorities constructed a carriage road

35 AE, NS, Turquie 105, P. Bambino (Beyrouth), 20 Nov. 1897.
36 Ibid.; AE, CC, Damas 6, Gilbert, 14 Sept. 1879; Lewis, *Nomads*, 67–93.
37 Guys, *Esquisse*, 220.
38 AE, CC, Damas 4, Hecquard, 16 Oct. 1862.
39 France, *Bulletin consulaire français* (1879), 646.
40 Great Britain, *Parliamentary Papers* (1889) 81:104.
41 France, *Bulletin consulaire français* (1885), 569–571.
42 See James A. Reilly, "Damascus Merchants and Trade in the Transition to Capitalism," *Canadian Journal of History* 27 (1992): 1–27.

linking Hama to Homs and the port of Tripoli in the mid-1880s.[43] Another road was under construction by the mid-1890s to join Hama with the port of Latakia via Qadmus in the Nusayri mountains.[44] The Hama–Homs–Tripoli road was in turn supplanted by a French-built railroad that joined Hama to Homs and Rayaq (a junction for Beirut and Damascus) in 1902, and to Tripoli in 1911.[45] Its status as a 'small district town' notwithstanding, Hama's commercial links with Ottoman – and eventually world – markets were a noteworthy facet of its economic activity. These Ottoman and international markets were outlets for the raw materials produced in Hama's hinterland and for the manufactures of its craft workers.

Hama's trade expanded commensurate with that of Syria as a whole. By mid-century Hama and Homs were exporting olive oil, sesame, cotton, silk, wool, grain, gall-nuts, madder roots and beeswax to Marseilles; and were importing French cloths and colonial products.[46] Hama's foreign trade developed to such a degree that France appointed a consular agent for the Homs and Hama district in 1853.[47] The growth of Tripoli's trade in the nineteenth century was closely linked to the port's accessibility to the adjoining interior regions of Hama and Homs.[48] The opening of the French rail line from Beirut to Hama in 1902 underlines the relatively greater importance to Hama of the littoral trade routes and their significance to the Ottoman authorities, French investors and the French government.[49]

The conquest of the steppe and the extension of modern communications affected different economic sectors and interests unevenly. The development of an internal and overseas grain market worked mainly to the benefit of Hama's landowners, who consoli-

43 Cuinet, *Syrie*, 125; As'ad, *Tarikh Hims*, 2:384.

44 Cuinet, *Syrie*, 125, 154–155, 161, 360.

45 As'ad, *Tarikh Hims*, 2:384–385.

46 AE, CC, Damas 3, de Gouy, Damas, 29 April 1853. Note the presence of 'Frankish cloth' (*shala afranjiyya*) among the possessions of a Hama woman in 1851. LCR Hama 53:156, 24 Dhu al-Hijja 1267/ 20 Oct. 1851.

47 AE, CC Damas 3, de Barrère, Damas, 6 Dec. 1853.

48 France, *Bulletin consulaire français* (1885), 569.

49 AE, NS Turquie 323, letter from President du Conseil of the Finance Ministry to the Foreign Minister, 4 February 1905.

dated their hold over newly settled lands. Growth in the volume of trade between Hama, the port of Tripoli, and Hama's hinterland was good news for merchants who plied these routes. Unlike the case of the trading relationship between Damascus and Beirut (where Christians dominated the export trade and Muslims the regional trade),[50] there does not seem to have developed in Hama a confessional division of labor between merchants who dealt in different markets. The absence of economic differentiation along confessional lines, combined with the low profile of European merchants and consuls in Hama, contributed to the maintenance of tranquillity between Muslims and Christians at a time when confessional tensions were rising in other parts of Syria as an indirect consequence of the country's integration into the world economy. The principal representative of French interests in Hama at mid-century was a commission agent for French firms in Tripoli, a Maronite Christian consular protégé named Faddul Bambino. His family had been associated for at least two decades with French interests and commerce between Marseilles and the Levant.[51] In 1852 Bambino was nominated French consular agent in Homs and Hama, and he took up residence in Hama where he was already involved in trade and commerce.[52] His activities in Hama progressed from commercial speculation and money-lending in the 1850s (e.g. to the minor notable Muhammad Efendi al-Sharabi), to a partnership with a Kurdish agha in the transport and sale of sheep in the 1860s, to agriculture and land speculation in the 1870s.[53] He enriched himself as an intermediary in Hama's trade via Tripoli with France, but he did not represent a kind of Christian mercantile sector in Tripoli corresponding to that emerging in Beirut at about the same time. Therefore, regardless of the enemies that he made or resentments that he aroused (and the French records accuse local officials of

---

50 Fawaz, *Merchants and Migrants*, 96; Reilly, "Damascus Merchants," 11–12.

51 AE, CC, Tripoli de Syrie 18, W. Guys, 20 Oct. 1828; CC, Beyrouth 1 bis, attached to Jorelle, 15 Jan. 1832; CC, Damas 3, de Barrère, 2 Nov. 1853.

52 AE, CC, Damas 3, de Gouy, 22 Oct. 1852.

53 AE, CC, Damas 3, de Barrère, 2 Nov. 1853; CC, Damas 5, Robin, 8 Aug. 1872; Great Britain, Foreign Office (FO) 78/1537, Brant to Bulwer, 8 April 1860; FO 78/1929, Rogers, 10 Feb. 1866; LCR Hama 53:362, 2 Muharram 1269/ 16 Oct. 1852.

intriguing against him on land issues),[54] Bambino's activities do not appear to have affected inter-confessional relations. There is little evidence that Bambino became personally identified with the Christian community in Hama, or acted as their patron or putative 'protector.' (Indeed, local Christians were among those who accused Bambino of fraudulent land dealings.)[55] Even among his French associates, Bambino's name could evince a certain reserve, suggesting that local French officials did not always have full confidence in him.[56] Homs and Hama were not at the top of French priorities, and this boded well for their inter-confessional relations. These contrasts help to explain the peacefulness of Muslim–Christian relationships in Hama at a time when social and economic tensions gave rise to confessional violence in Mount Lebanon, Damascus, and elsewhere in the Ottoman Syrian lands.[57]

Manufacturing in Hama felt the impact of Syria's integration into Eurocentric circuits of trade. By the end of the Ottoman period Syria as a whole, and the district of Hama in particular, imported significant quantities of manufactured products from European sources, including textiles, yarn and metal goods that competed with local craft production.[58] Artisans in Hama as elsewhere in Syria adapted to the economic changes of the nineteenth century and worked to advance or defend their interests. For instance, to compensate for the loss of a luxury market (as wealthy Syrians increasingly preferred foreign-manufactured goods),[59] Syrian manufacturers concentrated on the lower end of the market and produced goods to meet popular needs

---

54 AE, CC, Damas 5, Robin, 8 Aug. 1872.

55 Abdul-Karim Rafeq, "Ownership of Real Property by Foreigners in Syria, 1869–1873," paper presented to the Harvard Land Workshop, Harvard University, March 1–3, 1996.

56 Guys, *Esquisse*, 221; AE, CC, Damas 5, Robin, 11 Jan. 1873.

57 James A. Reilly, "Inter-Confessional Relations in Nineteenth-Century Syria: Damascus, Homs and Hama Compared," *Islam and Muslim-Christian Relations* 7 (1996): 213–224.

58 E.g. Ernest Weakley, *Report upon the Conditions and Prospects of British Trade in Syria* (London, 1911), 22, 135–181; France, *Moniteur officiel du commerce*, vol. 21 (1893), 70; vol. 62 (1914), 178.

59 E.g. As'ad, *Tarikh Hims*, 2:412.

and tastes.[60] The improvement in communications by road and rail encouraged the growth of a wider internal market in both manufactures and agricultural products.[61] Although by the mid-nineteenth century English yarn had replaced locally spun threads, English textiles had not replaced those of local manufacture which continued to enjoy strong local demand.[62] Syrian markets were important for Hama's textiles throughout the rest of the century even though they faced stiff competition from European imports.[63]

The continued importance of textile manufacturing in Hama notwithstanding, much remains unknown about changes within this industry in the nineteenth century. Some clues may be obtained from the experiences of other Syrian manufacturing centers. Local entrepreneurs sought to reduce costs and to keep a competitive edge over European imports by appealing to local tastes and responding quickly to changes in fashion. In addition, cloth merchants in Damascus and Homs founded associations to promote indigenous products over foreign ones.[64] Such developments attest to the flexibility and adaptability of local manufacture, but they exacted a price. Protective guild structures that had regulated prices, quality, and production fell by the wayside, and with them vanished subsistence guarantees that the guild structures had provided.[65] No data exist for Hama to demonstrate if weavers earned less, in constant terms, at the end of the nineteenth century than at the beginning, but global competition and price fluctuations made their livelihoods more perilous. Similarly, the fate of female spinners is difficult to determine. In the early part of the nineteenth century most Syrian spinners were women who worked at

---

60 These issues are discussed for Damascus's bellwether textile industry in James A. Reilly, "From Workshops to Sweatshops: Damascus Textiles and the World-Economy in the Last Ottoman Century," *Review* 16 (1993): 199–213.

61 Muhammad 'Ali Basha, *Rihla*, 142.

62 Guys, *Esquisse*, 220.

63 Cuinet, *Syrie*, 366–367.

64 As'ad, *Tarikh Hims*, 2:411–412; Reilly, "Workshops," *passim*.

65 Sherry Vatter, "Journeyman Textile Weavers in Nineteenth-Century Damascus: A Collective Biography," in *Struggle and Survival in the Modern Middle East*, ed. Edmund Burke III (Berkeley, 1993), 75–90.

home, but imports of English cotton threads disrupted this source of their income. The division of labor by gender meant that women were disproportionately hard hit by the influx of English threads from the mid-nineteenth century onward.[66] It is possible that women who once had spun shifted to textile piece-work at home or to paid agricultural labor in the fields, but they may have experienced a difficult transition between the demise of local spinning and its replacement by other types of work.[67] Finally, the loss of the luxury market to European goods and the marketing of local products to a poorer clientele meant that Syrian goods, including those of Hama, suffered a decline in quality and were not particularly remunerative by the early twentieth century.[68]

In these respects Hama, like other towns of the Syrian interior, preserved the form of its pre-industrial economy but in a new context represented by the integration of the Ottoman Empire into the world economy, and the transformation of the Empire into a semi-colonial modern state. Hama's manufactures found wider regional markets due to steamships and railroads; likewise its agriculture expanded and formed the basis of a new landowning class. When an Egyptian aristocrat – Ibrahim Pasha's grandson – visited Syria in 1910 he extolled Syrians' fealty to 'traditional' ways and forms. But the fact that he made his way by French-built rail, and was received (in Homs) by Christians espousing an Arabist cultural consciousness, suggests the depths of the changes that Syrians were experiencing.[69] Likewise the local history authored by Shaykh Ahmad al-Sabuni, who published a newspaper during the Young Turk period, reflected new currents when he criticized Hama's parochialism and worked to instill a 'modern' consciousness among his contemporaries.[70] Tradition that is conscious of itself as such is not truly traditional, in the sense that

66 Guys, *Esquisse*, 220.
67 Reilly, "Women," 94.
68 al-Sabuni, *Tarikh Hamah*, 118; Muhammad 'Ali Basha, *Rihla*, 142.
69 Muhammad 'Ali Basha, *Rihla*, 136–140.
70 al-Sabuni, *Tarikh Hamah*, 118.

the older forms can no longer merely be taken for granted. The form of Hama's economy in 1914 remained pre-industrial, but its context was very much that of the modern age.

Chapter Seven: Conclusion

This study of the social history of Ottoman Hama demonstrates that, in many respects, Hama may be studied as a microcosm of urban Syria. Hama's experience reflects the broader changes and transformations that characterized the Syrian lands in the later Ottoman period.

Structures and Hierarchies of Social and Political Power

The classical Ottoman Empire was transparently and unabashedly hierarchical. Its laws and institutions differentiated between rulers and ruled, between free persons and slaves, between Muslims and non-Muslims, and between nobles and commoners. The blurred or cross-cutting nature of some of these divisions created a degree of fluidity in the Ottoman social structure, but the principle of social and legal hierarchy and inequality was firmly established. This order of things was not seriously called into question until the Tanzimat reform era of the mid-nineteenth century.

In Hama families of elites and notables epitomized these hierarchies. By virtue of their military rank and status (agha, bey, pasha) or noble lineage (*ashraf*), certain individuals and families laid claim to power and status, subject to sultanic endorsement or acquiescence. Elites and notables were at the centers of patronage and social networks that tied them to urban society and to each other. The association of the elite ʻAzms and the noble Kaylanis, cemented by marriage and political alliances, was enduring and benefited members of both lineages. Urban quarters, merchants, and craft corporations relied on the patronage, support, and protection of their elite and notable patrons. Lesser elites and notables formed networks (including marital alliances) of their own. Elites owed their ascendancy to their connections to the Ottoman state, forming a kind of 'aristocracy of service.' Notables, in addition to their connection with the state, possessed autonomous cultural capital that flowed from their illustrious ancestry, their religious learning, and their association with mosques and Sufi lodges that they or their ancestors had founded.

Local Power Brokers and the Ottoman Center

Notable and elite families formed the power structures of Hama and dominated its economic life. On one level local and imperial authority was interdependent: the overall structure of power that allowed elites and notables to thrive was tied to Ottoman suzerainty, and Hama's well-being depended to a significant extent on its location along a major imperial road. On the other hand, though, the Ottomans (or at least Ottoman officials) were identified with oppression, misrule, onerous taxation and the imposition of forced loans. In this context successful elites and notables whose status was embedded both within local networks and the Ottoman imperial system performed a delicate balancing act. They were expected to defend as best they could the interests of local people against arbitrary Ottoman actions and demands.

The leading notable families of 'Alwani and Kaylani represented an urban-Islamic ethos. Their cultural capital as Sufis and *ashraf* gave them potential moral authority vis-à-vis representatives of the state. The Ottoman authorities needed the notables at least as much as the notables needed them. Because of their status as hereditary notables, the 'Alwanis, Kaylanis, and other *ashraf* were not entirely dependent on official patronage for their local prominence. At the same time, however, these notables usually worked with Ottoman authority to ensure that the leading religious and judicial posts were in the hands of local worthies. Their cooperation with the Ottomans helped to legitimize Ottoman rule and enabled the Ottomans' writ to run in Hama. At the same time, these notables could afford to maintain a certain critical distance from military governors and their excesses, representing (through their identification with Islamic law and the institution of the *shari'a* court) the ideal of 'justice.' The Ottoman aristocracy of service also blended with local society. Originally non-Arab families of Turkish and Kurdish origin like the 'Azms, Tayfurs and Barazis became assimilated into Hama's Arab society. A functional division of labor emerged: the military elites busied themselves with control of the countryside, maintenance of trade routes, and appropriation of the surpluses and profits therefrom; while the *ashraf* were linked to merchants and craft production – the 'urban economy' proper, so to speak. The creation of business and political partnerships between notables and elites consolidated the local structure of wealth and authority in Hama under the umbrella of Ottoman rule and within the Ottoman system.

Connections among Townspeople, Villagers, and Bedouins

Hama's economy was 'traditional' in the sense of being pre-industrial, but it was by no means simple or unchanging. In fact, the town played an important role as a center for processing the industrial and food crops of its hinterland, and for trade with the bedouins of the steppes. The importance of bedouins to Hama's economy, whether as suppliers, buyers, or business partners, underscores how significant and multi-faceted was the relationship between 'the desert and the sown.' A large part of Hama's regional trade existed because of the presence, production, and demand of the pastoralists, as the growth of al-Hadir quarter testifies.

Hama's pre-industrial economy was drawn into the new economic patterns of the nineteenth century. These were characterized by an extension of cereal cultivation in response to regional and international demand, and the accelerated export of raw commodities to Europe via Tripoli, and of manufactured goods to Ottoman and Egyptian markets. In this context 'pre-industrial,' sometimes called traditional, did not mean unchanging, unvarying, or stagnant. Hama-based landlords, as well as merchants dealing with the port of Tripoli, saw an upswing in their fortunes during the second half of the nineteenth century.

Consolidation of a Landowning Class

Those who were best positioned to take advantage of these new forces and economic changes were the elites and notables who already had established themselves as local power brokers. The major expansion of cultivated land in the second half of the nineteenth century spurred the formation of landed estates, a process that gave Hama its twentieth-century reputation as a city of big landlords. Those who were best placed to take advantage of these developments were elites with strong rural connections – the military families of ‘Azm, Tayfur, and Barazi – and the notable family of the Kaylanis who had long been associated with the ‘Azms and with the cultural, political and economic life of the town. Ottoman administrative reforms – specifically, the creation of local councils – gave these elite and notable families a formal vehicle of political expression for the consolidation of and defense of their local position and interests.

Hama, which appeared to twentieth-century observers as a bastion of tradition and of landlord feudalism, acquired these characteristics only during the nineteenth century. The emergence of Hama’s landed families was the last phase in a process by which selected notable and elite families combined to consolidate the resources of Hama district, exploiting their long association with the Ottoman state and the new market conditions of the nineteenth century. ‘Traditional’ Hama on the eve of the First World War was the product of modern processes whose roots went back just a couple of centuries. Like the rest of geographic Syria, Hama was already undergoing a significant transition prior to the dismantling of the Ottoman empire and the creation of new colonial states.

The agricultural character of Hama’s consolidated local elite may help to explain the conservative image that came to envelop them and their town. Hama was less touched than was its neighbor Homs by the currents of reformism and Arabism that animated many among Syria's educated classes in the last Ottoman years. It is perhaps no coincidence that merchant and manufacturing interests played a relatively greater role in the local leadership of Homs than of Hama, and that Homs was more open to the wider world because of communities of its merchants and émigrés in Egypt and the Americas. The most celebrated political figure from the Hama electoral district in the second Ottoman constitutional period (1908–1918), the Arabist parliamentarian 'Abd al-Hamid al-Zahrawi (d.1915), was in fact the scion of a notable family of Homs.[1] In the decades that followed, the local leadership of Hama were to be cast in the role of waging rear-guard actions against the various forms of social mobilization that the disruptions of war and colonial rule would unleash. The landlord-administrators of Hama, products and heirs of the Ottoman system, would come face to face with the French Mandate authorities in a duel for political control. Ironically, it was a struggle that both of them ultimately would lose.

1 Eliezer Tauber, *The Emergence of the Arab Movements* (London, 1993), 99, 290; al-Zahrawi, *Usur Hims*, 3:71–72; 112–114; As'ad, *Tarikh Hims*, 2:384–385; 411–412; 418–423; Muhammad 'Ali Basha, *Rihla*, 136–137.

Appendices

Appendix 1
Quarters Ranked by Tax Assessments (Piasters), 1730s & 1800

Shawwal 1144/April 1732 (tax collected)		Safar 1145/July 1732 (tax assessed)	
al-Hadir	364	al-Hadir	550
al-ʻAlaylat	310	al-ʻAlaylat	450
al-Nasara	200	al-Nasara	270
Dar al-Ghanam	170	Dar al-Ghanam	200
al-Dibagha	150	al-Dibagha	170
al-Mahaliba	100	Taht al-Shajara	140
al-Murabit	100	al-Murabit	130
al-Muʻtazala	100	al-Mahaliba	120
Taht al-Shajara	100	al-Muʻtazala	120
al-Barudiyya	80	Bab al-Qibli	100
al-Farra'in	76	al-Barudiyya	100
al-Bashura	56	al-Farra'in	100
Danuk maʻHawarina	52	Danuk maʻHawarina	80
al-Mashariqa	50	al-Bashura	80
Bab al-Jisr	40	al-Mashariqa	80
Bab al-Qibli	40	al-Safsafa	75
al-ʻAqiba	34	al-ʻAqiba	60
Nahr al-Junayna	24	Bab al-Jisr	60
al-Jaʻabira	20	al-Jaʻabira	40
al-Safsafa	[torn]	Nahr al-Junayna	40

SOURCES: LCR Hama 42:330, doc. 668, 19 Shawwal 1144/ 15 April 1732; 42:359, doc. 729, 3 Safar 1145/ 26 July 1732; 42:388, doc. 776, 23 Shawwal 1145/ 8 April 1733; 46:376, doc. 672, awasit Ramadan 1214/ 10 Feb. 1800.

Shawwal 1145/April 1733 (tax collected)		Ramadan 1214/Feb. 1800 (tax assessed)	
al-Hadir	569	al-ʻAlaylat	1700
al-ʻAlaylat	461	Bab al-Jisr	1700
Dar al-Ghanam	310	Bab al-Qibli	1700
al-Nasara	277	al-Bashura	1700
al-Dibagha	160	Bayn al-Hayrayn	1700
Taht al-Shajara	145	Dar al-Ghanam	1700
al-Murabit	138	al-Dibagha	1700
al-Mahaliba	125	al-Jarajima bi-Junayna wa-Nahr	1700
al-Muʻtazala	124		
al-Safsafa	107	al-Mahaliba	1700
Bab al-Qibli	105	al-Safsafa	1700
al-Barudiyya	103	al-Shamaliyya	1700
al-Hawarina wa-al-Danuk	84	Zuqaq al-ʻAsira	1700
al-Bashura	84	al-Muʻtazala	1150
al-Farra'in	82	al-Hawarina	850
al-Mashariqa	82	al-Jaʻabira	850
al-ʻAqiba	63	Taht al-Shajara	850
Nahr al-Junayna	46	al-Zanbaqi wa-al-Jura	850
al-Jaʻabira	42	al-Barudiyya	750
		al-Murabit	750
		al-Farra'in	650
		al-Mashariqa	650

Appendix 2
Hama's 26 Quarters (Mahallat), Early 20th Century

Left Bank (al-Suq)	**Right Bank (al-Hadir)**
Bab al-Jisr (south of river)	Bab al-Jisr (north of river)
al-Bashura (old citadel entrance)	Bayn al-Hayrayn
al-Dibagha (former tannery)	al-Shamaliyya
al-Madina	al-Sakhana
al-Bab al-Qibli	al-'Asida
al-Jarajima (old Bab al-Maghar)	al-Zanbaqi wa-al-Jura
al-Wadi (part of al-Jarajima)	al-Barudiyya
al-Ja'abira	al-Sharqiyya (old al-Mu'tazala)
Suq al-Shajara (Taht al-Shajara)	al-Jadida
al-Hawarina (part of al-Shajara)	al-Manakh
Dar al-Ghanam	
al-Mahaliba	
al-Mashariqa	
al-Faraya	
Jurat Hawa (old al-Safsafa)	
al-Murabit	
al-'Alaylat (the largest mahalla)	

SOURCE: al-Shaykh Ahmad al-Sabuni, *Tarikh Hamah* (Hama, 1956), 97, 100–101.

Select Bibliography

Primary Sources

Archival

France. Ministère des Relations Extérieurs. Correspondance commerciale et consulaire.

France. Ministère des Relations Extérieurs. Nouvelle série. Correspondance politique et commerciale.

Great Britain. Foreign Office. Reports of Consuls from Damascus and Beirut.

Syria. Directorate of Antiquities and Museums, Historic Documents Center (Suq Saruja). Islamic Law Court Registers of Hama.

Published

A Journey from Aleppo to Damascus. London: W. Mears et al., 1736.

Bell, Gertrude L. *Syria: The Desert and the Sown*. London: William Heinemann, 1907.

Bowring, John. *Report on the Commercial Statistics of Syria*. London: William Clowes & Sons, 1840; reprint ed., New York: Arno Press, 1973.

Burckhardt, John Lewis. *Travels in Syria and the Holy Land*. London: John Murray, 1822.

Cuinet, Vital. *Syrie Liban et Palestine: géographie administrative, statistique, descriptive et raisonnée*. Paris: Ernest Leroux, 1896.

France. Ministère de l'Agriculture et du Commerce; Ministère du Commerce, de l'Industrie et des Colonies. *Bulletin consulaire francais: recueil des rapports commerciaux addressés au Ministère des Affaires Etrangères*. Paris: Imprimerie Nationale, 1877–1891.

Great Britain. Foreign Office. *Trade Reports (Annual Series)*.

Great Britain. House of Commons. *Parliamentary Papers (Annual Series)*.

Guys, Henry. *Esquisse de l'état politique et commercial de la Syrie*. Paris: Chez France, 1862.

Lyde, Samuel. *The Ansyreeh and Ismaeleeh: A Visit to the Secret Sects of Northern Syria*. London: Hurst and Blackett, 1853.

al-Makki, Muhammad. *Tarikh Hims*. Edited and introduced by 'Umar Najib al-'Umar. Damascus: Institut Français d'Etudes Arabes de Damas, 1987.
Mishaqa, Mikha'il. *Muntakhabat min al-Jawab 'ala Iqtirah al-Ahbab*. 2nd ed. Edited by Asad Rustum and Subhi Abu Shaqra. Beirut: al-Maktaba al-Bulusiyya, 1985.
Muhammad 'Ali Basha. *al-Rihla al-Shamiyya*. Beirut: Dar al-Ra'id al-'Arabi, 1981.
al-Nabulsi, 'Abd al-Ghani ibn Isma'il. *al-Haqiqa wa-al-Majaz fi al-Rihla ila Bilad al-Sham wa-Misr wa-al-Hijaz*. Cairo: al-Hay'a al-Misriyya al-'Amma li-al-Kitab, 1986.
Porter, J. L. *The Giant Cities of Bashan, and Syria's Holy Places*. London: T. Nelson & Sons, 1866.
Robinson, George. *Voyage en Palestine et en Syrie*. 2 vols. Paris: Arthus Bertrand, 1838.
Volney, Constatin François. *Travels through Syria and Egypt*. 2nd ed. 2 vols. London: G. G. J. and J. Robinson, 1788.

Secondary Sources

Published

Abdel Nour, Antoine. *Introduction à l'histoire urbaine de la Syrie ottomane.* Beirut: Publications de l'Université Libanaise, 1982.
Abu-Husayn, Abdul-Rahim. *Provincial Leaderships in Syria 1575–1650.* Beirut: American University of Beirut, 1985.
Aricanli, Tosun and Mara Thomas. "Sidestepping Capitalism: On the Ottoman Road to Elsewhere." *Journal of Historical Sociology* 7, no. 1 (March 1994): 25–48.
As'ad, Munir al-Khuri 'Isa. *Tarikh Hims*. Vol. 2. Homs: The Orthodox Archbishopric, 1984.
al-'Azm, 'Abd al-Qadir. *al-Usra al-'Azmiyya.* Damascus: Matba'at al-Insha', 1960.
Baer, Gabriel. *Egyptian Guilds in Modern Times*. Jerusalem: The Oriental Society, 1964.
Barkey, Karen. *Bandits and Bureaucrats: The Ottoman Route to State Centralization.* Ithaca: Cornell University Press, 1994.
Batatu, Hanna. *The Old Social Classes and the Revolutionary Movements of Iraq: A Study of Iraq's Old Landed and Commercial Classes and of its Communists, Ba'thists, and Free Officers.* Princeton: Princeton University Press, 1978.
Chatterjee, Partha. *The Nation and its Fragments: Colonial and Postcolonial Histories*. Princeton: Princeton University Press, 1993.
Chevallier, Dominique. *Villes et travail en Syrie du XIXe au XXe siècle*. Paris: G.-P. Maisonneuve & Larose, 1982.

Clancy-Smith, Julia A. *Rebel and Saint: Muslim Notables, Populist Protest, Colonial Encounters (Algeria and Tunisia, 1800–1904)*. Berkeley: University of California Press, 1994.
Cohen, Amnon. *Economic Life in Ottoman Jerusalem*. Cambridge: Cambridge University Press, 1989.
Doumani, Beshara. "Endowing Family: Waqf, Property Devolution, and Gender in Greater Syria, 1800 to 1860." *Comparative Studies in Society and History* 40 (1998): 3–41.
—. *Rediscovering Palestine: Merchants and Peasants in Jabal Nablus, 1700–1900*. Berkeley: University of California Press, 1995.
Douwes, Dick. "Knowledge and Oppression: The Nusayriyya in the Late Ottoman Period." In *La Shî'a Nell'Impero Ottomano*, pp. 149–169. Rome: Accademia Nazionale del Lincei, 1993.
—. *The Ottomans in Syria: A History of Justice and Oppression*. London and New York: I. B. Tauris, 2000.
Douwes, Dick and Norman N. Lewis. "Taxation and Agriculture in the District of Hama, 1800–1831: New Material from the Records of the Religious Court." In *The Syrian Land in the 18th and 19th Century*, pp. 261–284. Edited by Thomas Philipp. Stuttgart: Franz Steiner, 1992.
Encyclopedia of Islam, 2nd ed. S.v. "Hamât" by D. Sourdel.
—. S.v. "Kâdiriyya" by D. S. Margoliouth.
—. S.v. "Rifâ'iyya" by C. E. Bosworth.
—. S.v. "Sa'diyya" by Barbara von Schlegell.
Establet, Colette and Jean-Paul Pascual. *Familles et fortunes à Damas: 450 foyers damascains en 1700*. Damascus: Institut Français d'Etudes Arabes, 1994.
Fawaz, Leila Tarazi. *Merchants and Migrants in Nineteenth-Century Beirut*. Cambridge, MA: Harvard University Press, 1993.
—. *An Occasion for War: Civil Conflict in Lebanon and Damascus in 1860*. Berkeley: University of California Press, 1994.
Fay, Mary Ann. "Women and Waqf: Toward a Reconsideration of Women's Place in the Mamluk Household." *International Journal of Middle East Studies* 29 (1997): 33–51.
Gerber, Haim. *Ottoman Rule in Jerusalem 1890–1914*. Berlin: Klaus Schwarz Verlag, 1985.
Ghazzal, Zouhair. *L'Economie politique de Damas durant le XIXe siècle: structures traditionelles et capitalisme*. Damascus: Institut Français d'Etudes Arabes de Damas, 1993.
Gibb, H. A. R. and Harold Bowen. *Islamic Society and the West: Islamic Society in the Eighteenth Century*. London: Oxford University Press, 1950.
Glasman, Vladimir. "Les documents du tribunal religieux de Hama: leur importance pour la connaissance de la vie quotidienne dans une petite ville de la Syrie centrale à l'époque ottomane." In *Les Villes dans l'Empire ottoman: activités et sociétés*, pp. 17–39. Edited by Daniel Panzac. Paris: CNRS, 1991.

Hamah: Ma'sat al-'Asr. [Lebanon]: The National League for the Liberation of Syria, 1983.

Hanioglu, M. Sükrü. "The Young Turks and the Arabs before the Revolution of 1908." In *The Origins of Arab Nationalism*, pp. 31–49. Edited by Rashid Khalidi et al. New York: Columbia University Press, 1991.

al-Hasani, 'Ali. *Tarikh Suriya al-Iqtisadi*. Damascus: Matba'at Bada'i' al-Funun, 1923–1924.

Holt, P. M. *Egypt and the Fertile Crescent 1516–1922: A Political History*. Ithaca NY: Cornell University Press, 1966.

Hourani, Albert. *A History of the Arab Peoples.* New York: Warner Books, 1992.

Ibsirli, Mehmet. "A Preliminary Study of the Public Waqfs in Homs and Hama in the XVIth Century." In *Studies on Turkish-Arab Relations Annual*, pp. 119–147. Istanbul: Foundation for Studies on Turkish-Arab Relations, 1986.

Islamoglu-Inan, Huri. *State and Peasant in the Ottoman Empire: Agrarian Power Relations and Regional Economic Development in Ottoman Anatolia during the Sixteenth Century*. Leiden: E. J. Brill, 1994.

Issawi, Charles. "Economic Change and Urbanization in the Middle East." In *Middle Eastern Cities: Ancient, Islamoic, and Contemporary Middle Eastern Urbanism. A Symposium*, pp. 102–121. Edited by Ira M. Lapidus. Berkeley: University of California Press, 1969.

—. *The Economic History of the Middle East 1800–1914*. Chicago: Chicago University Press, 1966.

Jwaideh, Albertine. "Aspects of Land Tenure and Social Change in Lower Iraq during Late Ottoman Times." In *Land Tenure and Social Transformation in the Middle East*, pp. 333–351. Edited by Tarif Khalidi. Beirut: American University of Beirut, 1984.

Khoury, Philip S. *Syria and the French Mandate: The Politics of Arab Nationalism 1920–1945*. Princeton: Princeton University Press, 1987.

—. *Urban Notables and Arab Nationalism: The Politics of Damascus 1860–1920.* Cambridge: Cambridge University Press, 1983.

Khuri, Fuad I. "The Alawis of Syria: Religious Ideology and Organization." In *Syria: Society, Culture, and Polity*, pp. 49–61. Edited by Richard T. Antoun and Donald Quataert. Albany: State University of New York Press, 1991.

Kunt, I. Metin. *The Sultan's Servants: The Transformation of Ottoman Provincial Government, 1550–1650.* New York: Columbia University Press, 1983.

Kurd 'Ali, Muhammad. *Khitat al-Sham*. 6 vols. Damascus: al-Matba'a al-Haditha, 1925–1928; reprint ed., Damascus: Maktabat al-Nuri, 1983.

Lapidus, Ira M. "Hierarchies and Networks: A Comparison of Chinese and Islamic Societies." In *Conflict and Control in Late Imperial China*, pp. 26–42. Edited by Frederic Wakeman, Jr. and Carolyn Grant. Berkeley: University of California Press, 1975.

—. “Muslim Cities and Islamic Societies.” In *Middle Eastern Cities: Ancient, Islamic, and Contemporary Middle Eastern Urbanism. A Symposium*, pp. 47–79. Edited by Ira M. Lapidus. Berkeley: University of California Press, 1969.
—. “Muslim Cities as Plural Societies: The Politics of Intermediary Bodies.” In *Urbanism in Islam: The Proceedings of the International Conference on Urbanism in Islam*, vol. 1, pp. 133–163. Edited by Takeshi Yukawa. Tokyo: The Middle Eastern Cultural Center, 1989.
Lewis, Norman N. *Nomads and Settlers in Syria and Jordan, 1800–1980.* Cambridge: Cambridge University Press, 1987.
Lovell, Mary S. *A Scandalous Life: The Biography of Jane Digby el Mezrab*. London: Richard Cohen Books, 1995.
Marcus, Abraham. “Men, Women and Property: Dealers in Real Estate in 18th Century Aleppo.” *Journal of the Economic and Social History of the Orient* 26 (1983): 137–163.
—. *The Middle East on the Eve of Modernity: Aleppo in the Eighteenth Century.* New York: Columbia University Press, 1989.
Marino, Brigitte. *Le Faubourg du Midan à Damas à l'époque ottomane: espace urbain, société et habitat (1742–1830).* Damascus: Institut Français d'Etudes Arabes de Damas, 1997.
Marsot, Afaf Lutfi al-Sayyid. *Women and Men in Late Eighteenth-Century Egypt*. Austin: University of Texas Press, 1995.
Masters, Bruce. *The Origins of Western Economic Dominance in the Middle East: Mercantilism and the Islamic Economy in Aleppo, 1600–1750.* New York: New York University Press, 1988.
—. “The 1850 Events in Aleppo: An Aftershock of Syria's Incorporation into the Capitalist World System.” *International Journal of Middle East Studies* 22 (1990): 3–20.
McChesney, R. D., translator. “Ilyas Qudsi on the Craft Organizations of Damascus in the Late Nineteenth Century.” In *A Way Prepared: Essays on Islamic Culture in Honor of Richard Bayly Winder*, pp. 80–106. Edited by Farhad Kazemi and R. D. McChesney. New York: New York University Press, 1988.
Meriwether, Margaret L. *The Kin Who Count: Family and Society in Ottoman Aleppo, 1770–1840.* Austin: University of Texas Press, 1999.
—. “Women and Economic Change in Nineteenth-Century Syria: The Case of Aleppo.” In *Arab Women: Old Boundaries, New Frontiers*, pp. 65–82. Edited by Judith E. Tucker. Bloomington: Indiana University Press, 1993.
Miura, Toru. “Personal Networks surrounding the Salihiyya Court in 19th Century Damascus.” In *Espace et société dans les villes arabes du Machreq à lépoque ottomane*. Damascus: Institut Francais d'Etudes Arabes de Damas, in press.
al-Muradi, Muhammad Khalil. *Silk al-Durar fi A'yan al-Qarn al-Thani 'Ashar*. 4 vols. Cairo: al-Matba'a al-Miriyya, 1874; reprint ed., Baghdad: Maktabat al-Muthna, 1966.

Musa, ‘Ali and Muhammad Harba. *Muhafazat Hamah: Dirasa Tabi‘iyya–Tarikhiyya–Bashariyya–Iqtisadiyya.* Damascus: Ministry of Culture, 1985.
Nu‘aysa, Yusuf Jamil. *Mujtama‘ Madinat Dimashq fi al-Fatra ma bayn 1186–1256 hijri 1772–1840 miladi.* 2 vols. Damascus: Dar Tlas, 1986.
Owen, Roger. *The Middle East in the World Economy, 1800–1914.* New York: Methuen, 1981.
Petran, Tabitha. *Syria.* London: Ernest Benn, 1972.
Quataert, Donald. “The Age of Reforms, 1812–1914.” In *An Economic and Social History of the Ottoman Empire*, pp. 759–943. Edited by Halil Inalcik with Donald Quataert. Cambridge: Cambridge University Press, 1994.
Rafeq, Abdul-Karim. “Al-fi’at al-ijtima‘iyya wa-milkiyyat al-ard fi bilad al-Sham fi al-rub‘ al-akhir min al-qarn al-sadis ‘ashar.” *Dirasat Tarikhiyya* no. 35–36 (March–June 1990), pp. 111–144.
—. *Buhuth fi al-Tarikh al-Iqtisadi wa-al-Ijtima‘i li-Bilad al-Sham fi al-‘Asr al-Hadith.* Damascus: By the Author, 1985.
—. “Craft Organization, Work Ethics, and the Strains of Change in Ottoman Syria.” *Journal of the American Oriental Society* 111 (1991): 495–511.
—. “Mazahir iqtisadiyya wa-ijtima‘iyya min liwa’ Hamah 942–943/1535–1536.” *Dirasat Tarikhiyya* no. 31–32 (March–June 1989), pp. 17–66.
—. “Qafilat al-hajj al-Shami wa-ahammiyatuha fi al-‘ahd al-‘uthmani.” *Dirasat Tarikhiyya*, no. 6 (1981), pp. 5–28.
—. *The Province of Damascus 1723–1783*. Beirut: Khayats, 1966.
Raymond, André. *Artisans et commerçants au Caire au XVIIIe siècle*. 2 vols. Damascus: Institut Français d’Etudes Arabes de Damas, 1973–1974.
—. *Grands villes arabes à l’époque ottomane*. Paris: Sindbad, 1985.
Reilly, James A. “Damascus Merchants and Trade in the Transition to Capitalism.” *Canadian Journal of History* 27 (1992): 1–27.
—. “From Workshops to Sweatshops: Damascus Textiles and the World-Economy in the Last Ottoman Century.” *Review* 16 (1993): 199–213.
—. “Inter-Confessional Relations in Nineteenth-Century Syria: Damascus, Homs and Hama Compared.” *Islam and Muslim-Christian Relations* 7 (1996): 213–224.
—. “Ottoman Authority and Local Society in Eighteenth-Century Hama.” *Arab Historical Review for Ottoman Studies* no. 13–14 (October 1996), pp. 123–134.
—. “Properties around Damascus in the Nineteenth Century.” *Arabica* 37 (1990): 91–114.
—. “Rural Waqfs of Ottoman Damascus: Rights of Ownership, Possession and Tenancy.” *Acta Orientalia* 51 (1990): 27–46.
—. “Status Groups and Propertyholding in the Damascus Hinterland, 1828–1880.” *International Journal of Middle East Studies* 21 (1989): 517–539.
—. “Urban Hegemony in the Hinterland of Ottoman Damascus: Villages, Estates and Farms in the Nineteenth Century.” In *Histoire économique et social de l’Empire ottoman et de la Turquie*, pp. 455–470. Edited by Daniel Panzac. Paris: Peeters, 1995.

—. "Women in the Economic Life of Late-Ottoman Damascus." *Arabica* 42 (1995): 79–106.

Rogan, Eugene L. *Frontiers of the State in the Late Ottoman Empire: Transjordan, 1850–1921*. Cambridge: Cambridge University Press, 1999.

Sabanu, Ahmad Ghassan. *Mamlakat Hamah al-Ayyubiyya*. Damascus: Dar Qutayba, 1984.

al-Sabuni, al-Shaykh Ahmad. *Tarikh Hamah.* Hama: al-Matba'a al-Ahliyya, 1956.

Schilcher, Linda Schatkowski. *Families in Politics: Damascene Factions and Estates in the 18th and 19th Centuries*. Stuttgart: Franz Steiner, 1995.

—. "The Hauran Conflicts of the 1860s: A Chapter in the Rural History of Modern Syria." *International Journal of Middle East Studies* 13 (1981): 159–79.

Shields, Sarah D. *Mosul before Iraq: Like Bees Making Five-Sided Cells*. Albany: State University of New York Press, 2000.

al-Siba'i, Muhammad 'Umar and Na'im Salim al-Zahrawi. *Hims: Dirasa Watha'iqiyya fi al-Hiqba min 1256–1337 h./ 1840–1918 m*. Part I. Homs: Matba'at al-Rawda, 1992.

Sjoberg, Gideon. *The Preindustrial City: Past and Present*. New York: The Free Press, 1960.

Sluglett, Peter and Marion Farouk-Sluglett. "The Application of the 1858 Land Code in Greater Syria: Some Preliminary Observations." In *Land Tenure and Social Transformation in the Middle East*, pp. 409–421. Edited by Tarif Khalidi. Beirut: American University of Beirut, 1984.

Tauber, Eliezer. *The Emergence of the Arab Movements*. London: Frank Cass, 1993.

Thompson, Elizabeth. "Ottoman Political Reform in the Provinces: The Damascus Advisory Council in 1844–45." *International Journal of Middle East Studies* 25 (1993): 457–475.

Toledano, Ehud R. *The Ottoman Slave Trade and its Suppression: 1840–1890*. Princeton: Princeton University Press, 1982.

Tucker, Judith E. *In the House of the Law: Gender and Islamic Law in Ottoman Syria and Palestine*. Berkeley: University of California Press, 1998.

—. "Taming the West: Trends in the Writing of Modern Arab Social History in Anglophone Academia." In *Theory, Politics and the Arab World: Critical Responses*, pp. 198–227. Edited by Hisham Sharabi. New York: Routledge, 1990.

Udovitch, Abraham L. *Partnership and Profit in Medieval Islam*. Princeton: Princeton University Press, 1970.

Vatter, Sherry. "Journeyman Textile Weavers in Nineteenth-Century Damascus: A Collective Biography." In *Struggle and Survival in the Modern Middle East*, pp. 75–90. Edited by Edmund Burke III. Berkeley: University of California Press, 1993.

Weulersse, Jacques. *L'Oronte: étude de fleuve.* Tours: Arrault, 1940.

—. *Le Pays des Alaouites*. Tours: Arrault, 1940.

—. *Paysans de Syrie et du Proche-Orient*. Paris: Gallimard, 1946.

al-Zahrawi, Na'im Salim. *Usur Hims wa-Amakin al-'Ibada min khuruj Ibrahim Pasha al-Misri wa-hatta khuruj al-'Uthmaniyyin al-Atrak, 1840–1918. Dirasa watha'iqiyya.* Vols. 2–3. Homs: Matba'at al-Fajr, 1995.
Zakariyya, Ahmad Wasfi. *'Asha'ir al-Sham*. 2nd ed. Damascus: Dar al-Fikr, 1983.
Ze'evi, Dror. *An Ottoman Century: The District of Jerusalem in the 1600s*. Albany: State University of New York Press, 1996.
Ziyada, Khalid. *al-Sura al-Taqlidiyya li-al-Mujtama' al-Madini: Qira'a Manhajiyya fi Sijillat Mahkamat Tarabulus al-Shar'iyya fi al-Qarn al-Sabi' 'Ashar wa-Bidayat al-Qarn al-Thamin 'Ashar.* Tripoli: Lebanese University, 1983.

Unpublished

Al-Dbiyat, Mohamed. "Homs et Hama en Syrie centrale: bipole ou doublet urbain?" Ph.D. dissertation, Université de Tours, 1992.
al-Qattan, Najwa. "The Historian at the Shari'a Court: Judging the Evidence Concerning Legal Practice." Paper presented at the 29th Annual Meeting of the Middle East Studies Association of North America, Washington DC, December 1995.
Barghuth, 'Abd al-Wadud Muhammad Yusuf. "Liwa' Hamah fi al-qarn al-sadis 'ashar: nizam al-hukm wa-bunyat al-mujtama' min sijillat al-mahkama al-shar'iyya bi-Hamah." M.A. thesis, 'Ayn Shams University, 1970.
Deguilhem-Schoem, Randi C. "History of Waqf and Case Studies from Damascus in Late Ottoman and French Mandatory Times." Ph.D. dissertation, New York University, 1986.
Douwes, Dick. "Justice and Oppression: Ottoman Rule in the Province of Damascus and the District of Hama, 1785–1841." Ph.D. dissertation, Catholic University of Nijmegen, 1994.
Meriwether, Margaret L. "The Notable Families of Aleppo, 1770–1830: Networks and Social Structure." Ph.D. dissertation, University of Pennsylvania, 1981.
Rafeq, Abdul-Karim. "Ownership of Real Property by Foreigners in Syria, 1869–1873," paper presented to the Harvard Land Workshop, Harvard University, March 1–3, 1996.
Roded, Ruth Michal. "Tradition and Change in Syria during the Last Decades of Ottoman Rule: the Urban Elite of Damascus, Aleppo, Homs and Hama, 1876–1918." Ph.D. dissertation, University of Denver, 1984.
Tomeh, Ramez George. "Landownership and Political Power in Damascus, 1858–1958." M.A. thesis, American University of Beirut, 1977.
Winter, Stefan. "The Nusayris before the Tanzimat in the Eyes of Ottoman Provincial Administrators." Paper delivered to the Syria-III conference, Erlangen, Germany, July 2000.
Yusuf [Barghuth], 'Abd al-Wadud Muhammad. "Tarikh Hamah fi al-qarn al-thamin 'ashar." Damascus?, n.d. (Typewritten MS at IFEAD library, Damascus.)

Index